also by jaycee dugard

a stolen life

freedom

my book of firsts

jaycee dugard

SIMON & SCHUSTER PAPERBACKS

New York   London   Toronto   Sydney   New Delhi

Simon & Schuster Paperbacks
An Imprint of Simon & Schuster, Inc.
1230 Avenue of the Americas
New York, NY 10020

First Simon & Schuster trade paperback edition July 2017

SIMON & SCHUSTER PAPERBACKS and colophon are
registered trademarks of Simon & Schuster, Inc.

For information about special discounts for bulk purchases,
please contact Simon & Schuster Special Sales at
1-866-506-1949 or business@simonandschuster.com.

The Simon & Schuster Speakers Bureau can bring authors
to your live event. For more information or to book an
event contact the Simon & Schuster Speakers Bureau at
1-866-248-3049 or visit our website at www.simonspeakers.com.

Manufactured in the United States of America

10 9 8 7 6 5 4 3 2 1

The Library of Congress has cataloged the hardcover edition as follows:

Names: Dugard, Jaycee Lee, 1980– | Dugard, Jaycee Lee, 1980– Stolen life.
Title: Freedom: my book of firsts / Jaycee Dugard.
Other titles: Freedom
Description: First Simon & Schuster hardcover edition. | New York : Simon &
    Schuster, 2016. | "Simon & Schuster nonfiction original hardcover"—Title
    page verso.
Identifiers: LCCN 2016016388 (print) | LCCN 2016017705 (ebook) | ISBN
    9781501147623 (hardcover) | ISBN 9781501147647 (ebook)
Subjects: LCSH: Dugard, Jaycee Lee, 1980– | Kidnapping victims—California—
    Biography. | Sexually abused children—California—Biography. | Young women—
    California—Biography. | Freedom. | Life skills. | Self-actualization (Psychology) |
    BISAC: BIOGRAPHY & AUTOBIOGRAPHY / Personal Memoirs. |
    BIOGRAPHY & AUTOBIOGRAPHY / Women. | SELF-HELP / Abuse.
Classification: LCC HV6574.U6 D8 2016 (print) | LCC HV6574.U6 (ebook) |
    DDC 364.15/4092 [B]—dc23
LC record available at https://lccn.loc.gov/2016016388

ISBN 978-1-5011-4762-3
ISBN 978-1-5011-4763-0 (pbk)
ISBN 978-1-5011-4764-7 (ebook)

I dedicate this book to my mom and all the
"moon moms" who hold on to hope!

Acknowledgments

I want to acknowledge the tremendous support and encouragement I had in even writing this book. I would like to thank my agent Mort Janklow and my publisher Jonathan for letting me, not once, but twice tell the story my way and for always believing I could, even if at times I had my doubts.

To my mom, who by example has taught me patience and unconditional love. To my aunt Tina, who continues to share the magic with me. To my sister, who shines from within and without whenever she walks into a room and who always tells me how proud she is of me—well, girl, I'm so proud of you, too! And to my two daughters, who give me gray hairs before I'm forty but constantly remind me what true resilience looks like: I'm so darn proud of you both.

I want to also acknowledge all of the people that have sent out their love protons to me and my family throughout our terrible/ grand adventure.

I want to thank Monkey and Nanny Goat for always having

my back and for giving me so much. I can't imagine my life without either one of you.

Last of all, I want to acknowledge and thank all the people that have gotten me to this place in my life. All the little moments add up; each one has helped shape me and tells a tale. I am so thankful to have you all in my inner circle of love.

Contents

contents

contents

contents

Introduction

You can't really be strong until you
see the funny side of things.
—ANONYMOUS

Hi again. For those who read my first book, *A Stolen Life*, I would like to thank you for your huge amount of support. Some of you, however—and you know who you are—still can't quite remember who I am. No, I am not a Duggar. I do not have eighteen siblings. Let's get one thing straight: my last name is DUGARD.

Many confuse me and my story with Elizabeth Smart. Just for the record, I am not Elizabeth Smart. Even though we both have blond hair, we have had vastly different lives and experiences. I am the one that was captive for EIGHTEEN YEARS! Not months. Not to say that what she went through wasn't as bad as what I did. I'm not comparing us, but some have.

Believe it or not, I have also been mistaken for one of the girls held captive by Ariel Castro in Cleveland. Apart from being held by a deranged man for a number of years, I'm not sure how I get confused with these brave ladies: Amanda Berry, Gina DeJesus, and Michelle Knight.

When I was first recovered, it was hard to put into words what I and my daughters had been through. I wasn't really the talkative type back then. Up until that point, Phillip had done most of the talking throughout the eighteen years of captivity, and it was mostly in the form of lectures and his idea of daily sermons. I mostly talked with the girls and that's it. So to have so many people to talk to all of a sudden was very overwhelming. I gave these men and women the bare essentials of what happened. It wasn't until I met Rebecca Bailey that I really wanted to open up.

I remember we were sitting in the backyard of the rental she and her team had found for us to stay in. Just the two of us. It was the first day we met. I told her right off I wasn't comfortable talking about what happened. The backyard we were in was all fenced in, but we could hear a neighbor working in the yard next door. After making my proclamation about not talking, she said that was fine. We just sat for second or two and all of a sudden, words started pouring out of my mouth. Maybe it was her willingness to just sit there with me. Or the fact I felt no judgment from her at all, but my whole life story just came tumbling out of me. Rebecca was actually trying to get me to stop at one point because she realized the noise from the neighbor had stopped and that there was an unmistakable hush from the other side and we knew someone's ears were burning. We both laughed at that point and decided it was time for a break. I had told her a lot, though. It went a little like this . . .

It all started on a bright and sunny day in South Lake Tahoe. I was eleven years old. It was an ordinary day just like countless others I had had in my short eleven years of life. Then everything changed for me and my family. I was walking up to the school bus stop when a car came up behind me and stopped at an angle in front of me. Cutting off any chance of an exit. I wasn't scared at first, though. I had no reason to be. Nothing could prepare me for what was to happen next.

The man in the driver's seat opened his window and started to ask me for directions. Before I could answer, he shoved his door open and stunned me with a stun gun. (I didn't know what it was at the time, just that it made me lose control of my arms and legs.) I fell back into some bushes. Stunned, I tried to scoot backward, but there was nowhere to go. Nowhere to hide from the terrible man coming for me. Dragging me to his car. I try to hold on to whatever I can to no avail. (Years later, during my recovery process I would remember that the last thing I touched was a pinecone on the ground. It would become my symbol of new beginnings and the logo of my foundation.) The man throws me in the backseat where another person is waiting for me and covers me with a heavy blanket. (Later I learned this was Nancy Garrido, Phillip Garrido's wife.) This person held me down. I felt like I couldn't breathe. I know I passed out at some point.

These events happened so many years ago. Even though I am well into my thirties now, I can still close my eyes and relive these events as if they just happened yesterday. These are moments ingrained into my psyche and cannot be erased. I choose to not let them take over my life now. And I choose to create new, better memories. Memories that will eventually outweigh these bad memories until they are nothing but dust in the air.

That was the longest car ride ever. I remember being so embarrassed that I had wet myself. I found out later that it was because of the stun gun he used. The details of my horrific and ultimately triumphant story can be found in my first book, *A Stolen Life*. My first book was a story that I needed to let people hear. To know it was not my shame but the shame of two people, Phillip and Nancy Garrido. It was therapeutic for me in many ways. I even wrote some of it in my therapy sessions with my therapist, Rebecca.

This second book is different. This is my new story. In it, I can be whoever I want to be. Not who someone wants me to be.

I've been asked this question many times throughout the year . . .

"Jaycee, how are you going to rebuild your life?" This question has stayed with me these past years. I didn't know how to answer it for a long time. I ask myself, Do I know now?

How do you make a life for yourself and your kids when you have no idea where to begin?

- How do you rebuild a life?
- Do you rebuild it on the notion of what you think it should have been? Do you rebuild on a life you once lived?
- How do I build a life I never thought I would live to see?

So many questions but no answers . . .

Today if someone asked me the same question, I would say: Hmmm . . . one day at a time.

One second at a time, one hour at a time, one day at a time, one month, one year . . . and all the little moments and people that go into building and living a new life of freedom and choices.

Is that an answer? I don't know, but in order to share my life with you, I have to build you a picture of all the moments that have gone into my life now. These moments have helped shape me, and I hope that the sharing of these moments shows what goes into creating a new life. These seemingly small moments are actually all very significant. Each one has helped me define within myself who I am now.

Do I wonder what my life would have been like if Phillip and Nancy Garrido never snatched me from my tranquil life? You bet your last dollar I do! But what's done is done. I can't take back what happened. I can only march quietly forward and forge a path on uncharted territory. I think I've done quite well. If I do say so myself. In fact, I don't really think I'm at all unique or special. I believe anyone could have survived what I went through. You just have to want to be okay. That's a choice I made. I wanted to be okay.

Was I okay overnight? No, it takes time. I believe in seeking help and counseling. It helps to have someone to talk to. That someone for me was Dr. Rebecca Bailey. She is the founder of Transitioning Families, a unique equine-based program that specializes in reunification.

My daughters had never met any of my family before. Likewise, even though I knew my mom and family, they had never met my daughters. It helped to have Rebecca and Jane, her cotherapist, there for us as a family. Jane became my ADL helper. ADL stands for activities of daily living. And trust me, I had missed out on learning a lot of the daily activities that are normal to everyone else. She helped me with things like balancing a checkbook, even helped me learn to grocery shop by myself. She continues to be an important person in my life.

We needed the guidance from this team to learn how to connect with each other. You might think, Hey, what's the big deal? You should be happy you were free. Of course I was! That was the big picture for us. The reality was that we were virtual strangers to each other. What seemed like fun exercises with her horses were actually teaching us the new skills we needed to form those lasting connections with each other. Chef Charles, Rebecca's husband and the cook for Transitioning Families, was a vital factor in our recovery process, too. Besides all the delicious new foods he was introducing us to, he was also one of the first males my daughters had been around other than their father. I think those early days helped them to see that men could be so much more than what they had witnessed their tyrannical, possessive, egotistical, egomaniacal, narcissistic, psychopathic father being. I think this has led them to have healthy relationships throughout these years of freedom.

It has not been easy. I can attest to that. But each moment has brought an emotion, a memory, a time to share, and a time for self. So many firsts . . . where to begin . . . First sight of my mom in eighteen years, first time meeting my grown-up sister Shayna, hugging my aunt Tina and us celebrating her birthday at Disneyland every year I have been back, first barbecue with the whole Dugard clan. Making the choice to have the girls attend school, first doctor visits, and first shared caramel-covered apples with Mom. Learning to drive and first car, first plane ride and reuniting with old friends. Some of these firsts were in my first book, *A Stolen Life*. All these years of freedom later, what's new with me? Let's find out . . .

Fly Me to the Moon

First time I flew in the plane I was six years old, and my mom had a boyfriend that was a pilot. I remember it was a little plane and I threw up. It wasn't the most fun I ever had for sure. I never flew again until eighteen years later, after my rescue.

The first time I flew in a big plane I was worried that same feeling of nausea would come back from my younger days. The chance to fly in a big plane far outweighed any fears I had, though, and I was looking forward to this new experience. I didn't want to think about being sick. I just wanted to fly!

Having a lot of time on my hands in the prison of Phillip and Nancy's backyard, I had a lot of time to dream and fantasize. One fantasy I had was having the ability to fly like Peter Pan. Often dreaming that with a little fairy dust I could fly myself home—

Poof! . . . Tinker Bell, where are you? I would cry. But she never came.

I also imagined myself flying from city to city as a flight attendant one day. I thought it would be so much fun to see the world in this way. From London to Paris. Rome, Italy, Egypt. I have always wanted to see the pyramids. I did get to see the Mayan ruins on a trip to Belize. A group of us went to help a tiny village called Monkey River rebuild after the devastating hurricane that they were still recovering from. While there, we explored a pyramid called Altun Ha which means "stone water." It was amazing and so big. Climbing to the top I felt like a queen. But I digress. I will tell you more of this story later.

This trip was to be my first meeting with Nancy Seltzer. Our need for protection from the media was an obvious priority from the beginning of our recovery. We needed the time to focus on each other and not the constant hounding of the media we were experiencing. Some people wanted to help, and we got involved with one in particular that we thought we could trust. It didn't end up that way, and we didn't know where to turn for help after that.

Rebecca wanted to help but had her hands full with not only our therapy needs but also dealing with all the agencies and law enforcement involved with the court case against Phillip and Nancy Garrido, our captors. Her brother-in-law, an actor, knew of our plight and suggested a woman that he trusted in the business of public relations. Rebecca passed this information on to me and, together with my mom, we contacted Nancy Seltzer and explained our story. We asked for her help and, thankfully, she agreed and the rest is history. She did what she said she would and protected us from the media and those who were seeking to exploit us.

On the day of my first flight, we were actually met in the airport parking lot by a security guard and taken through a special way to avoid any press that was lurking. My story was still new then and in high demand. I was accompanied on this trip by my mom and therapist Rebecca.

Once we boarded, I remember the flight attendant asking me if I was old enough to be sitting in the exit row. How funny she would ask, I thought. She said I looked like I was fifteen. No, I replied, I'm thirty! She was shocked. I don't look my age, apparently. Still don't to this day. The other day I was in Costco. They had the food samples out. I went to take one that looked like a health drink, and the lady at the booth stopped me and said, "You have to be over eighteen to drink that." What? Hello . . . I'm thirty-five! I also went to a wedding once and during the toast I was served Martinelli's sparkling apple juice instead of Champagne! I had even put on makeup! Come on, people, I am a grown-up! Anyways, I'm wandering again. The flight attendant did let me keep my seat.

Over the speaker system "Fly Me to the Moon," by Frank Sinatra came on. I looked at Mom, who was sitting beside me, and we shared a smile. Fly us to the moon, Frank, this is our song! That actually helped me to relax. Until we started to accelerate and actually take off. My hands and fingers dug into the armrest. My mom asked if I was okay, and with gritted teeth, I answered "Yep." Turns out, I was okay for the entire trip. I did some deep breathing and looked straight ahead the whole way. Landing made me queasy. I knew I had to take an airsickness pill next time. Rebecca recommended Dramamine. I have taken it ever since, and flights have become so much easier. I have also found a homeopathic remedy, MotionEaze, that works for me on short flights.

Nancy picked us up from the airport herself. Meeting her was like meeting an old friend. One that felt like I had known forever. Actually, with all the talks we had had over the phone up to that point, I really did feel like I already knew her and, most importantly, like I could trust her. So when we met face-to-face that day it felt comfortable. I knew she had our backs and would do all she could to protect me and my family from the prying eyes of the media. Her two beautiful dogs sealed the deal as they greeted us excitedly in the car. I knew right then she was a friend for life.

Later, getting to know Nancy, we decided she needed a nickname. Funny how a certain name can follow you. "Nancy" is that name for me. Although there has only been one "Bad Nancy," the new Nancy in my life wanted a name that didn't remind me of the old one. She said as a child she had had the nickname of Nanny Goat for her way of taking care of everyone she loved. So she became my Nanny Goat in more ways than one.

We stayed with Nanny Goat a few days. She introduced me to some people that would become very important in my life. One of them was Michael, who would take care of my finances, and another was Dale, who would represent me and my daughters in our lawsuit against the state. Our stay was very productive and a whole new experience of meeting people for me.

The flight back home was scheduled for nighttime, and we were a little late getting to our gate for the flight. As we walked through the tiny airport, I suddenly heard our names over the speakers. "Terry Probyn, Jaycee Dugard, Rebecca Bailey, please proceed to your gate." Rebecca looked scared as she ran ahead to ask them to stop. (Remember, the press was still hounding us. That very day a reporter from a tabloid had gone by Rebecca's house and asked where Rebecca was. The reporter told her fifteen-year-old who answered the door that he was with the FBI and needed to find her.) Guess what happened at the airport. No one even looked twice as our name was repeated over the loud-speaker again and again. Funny how I could be in plain sight and no one noticed!

I remember that day on the flight home, sitting there holding my mom's hand as we took off, and she said, "Look out the window." I said, "No I can't." I didn't want to be sick if I turned my head to look, and it was scary being so high up from the ground. My mom promised me I would like what I saw. I turned my head and opened my eyes. I realized I didn't feel sick, so I looked out a little more and I saw diamonds twinkling, shining bright, but not in the sky. They were below me. Beautiful sparkling diamonds on the ground and me looking high above them. I forgot to be scared in that moment. I had never seen such a magical display of twinkling lights, even more brilliant than the night sky. From then on, I couldn't wait for my next flight. I still have to take Dramamine, but I enjoy flying more because I remember those twinkling diamonds. Happy memories help when you're afraid. I always try for a window seat so I can look out over the world. I never get sick of the sight.

I've been on many flights now and I've even flown all by myself. The first time I flew by myself was actually a pretty fun adventure, even though I didn't think it was at the time. For a while the thought of traveling alone was really scary. What happened if I got lost? What if I got on the wrong plane and ended up in a strange city? What would I do then? My mom and sister encouraged me to try it but only when I was ready. My sister, again the little one teaching the older one, told me it would be fun to travel alone. She thought I was more than capable of handling any situation that came up. Encouragement like that is what helps the most in new situations and adventures.

I got the chance to take this advice and encouragement sometime later. I was coming back from a visit to my sister's house. My mom was staying a few extra days, and I was planning on going on my first solo flight. I felt ready to face this new challenge.

The flight had a layover in Dallas. I had been on layovers before and knew the routine. The plane was late taking off, so I knew I had to run to my next flight when we landed. To prepare myself, I studied the magazine with the layout of the airport in it. I knew from previous flights that Dallas was a big airport with trains to take you from terminal to terminal. The first time I was in the Dallas airport the group I was traveling with got on the wrong train, and we ended up across the airport with five minutes to spare before our next flight. I was not going to do it again, especially not by myself! The man next to me saw me looking at the terminal layout and offered some helpful suggestions and helped me plot my course to the assigned gate. I was thankful because I would have been too shy to ask for help.

As soon as I was able to disembark, I ran for all I was worth to the gate assigned to my flight. I had checked my luggage, so I just had my purse and made good time. I even had to navigate the dreadful train. I finally made it to the correct gate only to find out that the gate had been changed! What the?! I ran to the next gate only to find out that my flight had been delayed anyway. Relieved but out of breath, I sat and realized that I needed to charge my phone because I had 10 percent power left. I walked to find an outlet to charge my phone. It was around 10:30 at night and my flight was rescheduled for 11:15 p.m. I thought I had a few minutes at least to charge my phone. (Why are iPhone batteries always running out when you need them the most?)

After charging for a bit, I decided to head back to my gate. Walking back, I became a little worried because the airport seemed deserted and some areas had cots out. Upon reaching my gate I saw there was nobody at the desk, actually nobody anywhere. Oh no, what should I do? I thought to myself, Don't panic. You can handle this. Like Dory says, "Just keep swimming, just keep swimming." I walked a few gates down and finally found somebody at a desk. I said, "Excuse me, but my flight was delayed and now there's nobody there. What happened?" She said, "Oh, the flight was canceled." Just like that, like it was no big deal. I'm in Dallas–Fort Worth and my flight has been canceled! I'm alone in some strange city airport! And where in the hell was my luggage? I felt like I couldn't handle it. But I knew there was nobody else to handle it for me. I was on my own and it felt . . . different.

I said, "Well, what am I going to do?" She didn't really answer me and acted like she didn't know. I didn't really know if I should repeat my question or just continue to stand there. As I stood there, she handed me a bunch of papers she had printed out. She called them vouchers. She explained that one was for dinner tonight in the airport (even though all the stands had closed for the night) and a taxi ride to the hotel. I'm thinking to myself, Oh my God, I'm going to have to go to a hotel by myself and take a cab ride! She went on to say that there was one for another cab ride back to the airport in the morning, one for breakfast, and a voucher for a standby flight. I took the tickets from her and walked to the exit.

Looking up at the airport exit sign felt like a turning point. "Exit your old life," it seemed to say. "Exit now and become . . . what?" Okay, I said to myself. Just keep swimming. I have never been so scared in my life . . . Well, that's not true. I had never been in this kind of situation before was all. It felt scary and new and different. Sometimes I have to remind myself what I have been through. People tell me I am strong, brave, etc. To be honest, I usually just tell myself I am lucky. How funny is that to think I'm lucky after everything I have been through.

But on that day I did not feel lucky at all—just annoyed, frustrated, tired, and a little scared. I left the relative safety I felt in the airport and entered a hot, muggy unpredictable night. It was past midnight by this time. I didn't know what I was supposed to do really, but luckily, there were a few taxis still outside at that time of night. I peeked in the open window and told the driver I had vouchers for a cab ride to this hotel in downtown Fort Worth. He said, "I can take you" in a heavy foreign accent. Okay, I told myself, this is going to be okay. Just stay alert. Be present. Stay in the moment. All things I had learned from Rebecca.

After what felt like hours of riding in a stranger's cab, I thought to myself, Where is he taking me? Does he know where to go? Is he taking me somewhere to rape and kill me? In reality, though, the ride to the hotel was probably no more than twenty-five to thirty minutes. I gave myself permission to have all these thoughts because I felt like if I thought about all the things that could happen, then they wouldn't. It's the things you don't think about that get you. Of course, nothing of the sort happened, but can you blame me for thinking of all the worst scenarios that could? How much bad luck can a girl have, though, right?

We arrived at the hotel. The cabdriver turned out not to be a serial killer but a very nice man. He asked if I would be returning to the airport in the morning and I said yes. He gave me his number and said to call when I was ready and he would pick me up. I thanked him and left the sanctuary of the cab to enter the jungle of a strange city. Well, it wasn't quite the jungle, and it actually felt pretty safe. I walked the few steps and entered the still brightly lit lobby of my hotel for the night. I showed the desk my voucher and they gave me a room. I navigated my way to the elevator and was relieved to have already learned how to easily find my hotel room. Room 202 so that would put me on the second floor. Wipe the sweat from my brow for figuring that out.

By the time I reached my room, I had to go to the bathroom something fierce. Mother Nature is not kind. I realized she had given me my monthly gift and I had bled through my pants. Mother Nature also gives us brilliant ideas to deal with problems such as these. Since I had checked my luggage and was wearing the only clothes I had, I would wash my pants in the sink and hang them to dry, for surely they would dry by morning. (Which I forgot was already here at one in the morning.) But sometimes things are overlooked in times of crisis. I washed my pants in the sink and got most of the stain out. I hung them over the shower rod to dry.

I ate the meager snacks I had from my first plane ride and fell asleep quickly. Only to be woken up an hour later to the sounds of yelling from the room next door. I must admit at first it startled me with thoughts of bullets flying through the wall. But I told myself again to just chill out and go back to sleep. I finally fell asleep again around 3:00 a.m. and woke the next morning to my alarm.

First thing I did was check my pants and yes, of course, they were still very, very damp. I had no other clothing to put on, so I put them on and tied my sweater around my waist. I called the number I had been given by the cabdriver the night before, and he said he would be there in fifteen minutes to pick me up. I got ready and went downstairs to meet him. By the time I got downstairs, there was a line of cabdrivers already in front of the hotel. One saw me and immediately descended upon me like I was some kind of tasty morsel for him to consume. I told him I had already called for a ride, but in their foreign language I don't know if they understood me. I kept saying, No, thank you, but he kept saying, No, that's not how it works. I was feeling very intimidated, so I called my cabdriver back and explained what was going on. He said, It's okay. Just go ahead and use the first cab in the line. I thanked him for his trouble and got into the cab. Who knew there was cab etiquette? I mean, shouldn't you just be able to get in any cab you want? So many rules to figure out sometimes. Why can't things just be simple?

On arriving back at the airport, I went into the security line thinking I had a plane ticket. The security officer informed me that I didn't have a ticket and said it was a voucher for a ticket and I needed to go to the airline desk. I went to the front desk and was told that I was going to be put on standby for the next available flight home. It came with a layover, too. Again what happened to simple? It turned out my flight had to go four hours in one direction and then back the same way two hours to get where I needed to go. It wasn't like I was going to a tiny airport, even. In fact, it was to a big airport in a major city. It seems like something is a little off in that thinking. The lady next to me told me she had taken a plane to a city in the Midwest and because of weather she had to land in a different city. She added that when she got to that city, the airline had to put her on a bus because they had no room on any planes to the city she actually needed to be in. She told me the bus ride took two hours and when she got there, she had to book a flight back to her car at the original airport where she was supposed to land. The airline had told her nowhere did her ticket say they had to fly her to her destination. I guess it might make sense to somebody, but it didn't to me. Five hours later, I finally arrived home, exhausted but very proud of myself.

OMG! Out in Public!

My first experience in an outdoor shopping mall was comical. Thinking about it now, I can easily see it being one of those funny skits on *Saturday Night Live*. It was during my first plane trip to meet Nancy. Nanny Goat took us out and we went to The Grove shopping center in LA. I was mesmerized as I was confronted by so many shops, food choices, and people. So many things to see and look at, I'm sure I'm not even remembering them all. I had my mouth open probably the whole time looking like the biggest fool. Maybe everybody thought I was catching flies or some crazy person who never closes her mouth. Yes, everybody! Because in my mind everyone was staring at me! Have you ever felt like everyone is staring at you? I really did for a while after my recovery. I was positive all eyes were on me all the time, yet I also felt invisible. Wow, what a contradiction I was!

I've grown a lot and feel some things are different for me now. I don't feel like all eyes are on me, more like I'm just another human being making her way in this world, like everyone else is doing. I remember the first few years into my recovery were difficult because I wanted to maintain my privacy for me and my family but at the same time live a normal life. I was trying to figure out what "normal" was going to be for me. With no reference and no road map. Going into any restaurant, especially when the girls went, too, always made me a wee bit nervous because I wanted their privacy protected above all else. I always worried about being recognized, so I would always make sure I positioned myself in a spot where the least amount of patrons could see my face. Why? I ask myself now. I guess I was worried they would act like the media and ask a hundred questions or want a photo or something. In all these years, that has never happened. If anyone did actually recognize me in a place with them, they were so polite about it, they never said anything. I appreciate those people. They allowed me to enter this brand-new world in a natural and less scary way. At least, in my own mind, what I thought scary would be. But I ask myself now and think, Would it have been as scary as I thought it would be?

It took time, but I eventually became comfortable going out and realized that, yes, we all become obsessed at times with the Kim Kardashians and the beautiful royal couple and enjoy talking about the people in the news. But at the end of the day nobody is sitting in a restaurant saying, "Look over there, Harriet. Is that Jaycee Dugard in the corner over there hiding behind that booth?" No, they are deep into conversations about soccer games, and dance recitals, who won the World Series and normal everyday life things. I find that I don't sit with my back to people now when I go out. In fact, I don't even think about it anymore. It wasn't a conscious decision I made one day but more of an unconscious one. I sit where I want, and that is certainly a great feeling to have.

In the big outdoor Grove mall that day, I'm sure I sounded like I was from another planet. With my endless questions like "Why is there a DJ playing in the middle of the mall?" "Yum, that funnel cake drenched in whipped cream and chocolate looks delish, can we get some?" and "Oh, my, how much does that jacket cost?"

Malls had changed so much since I was little. I remember malls being loud but not like this. The best part of malls for me was the pet shops! I loved going to the mall because that is where you could pet the little kittens, puppies, or bunnies in those open-top plastic boxes. Some shops even had benches that went all around the plastic boxes so little girls like me could follow the fluffy bunnies as they hopped around their small little world. Looking back, I feel sad for those little animals in those boxes. They remind me of me in the backyard. Helpless to do anything about their circumstances in life, just waiting for the right person to come along and take them from their little prisons. Back then, though, I was too naïve to even think that way or think that someone could become imprisoned the way I was years later. I remember I would get so pouty if they didn't have any animals in the mall when we went. Those were the days before PetSmart and Petco.

Now there are no more pets in the mall, but oh so many brand-new clothes and shoes! So many clothes I could hardly believe it! In the backyard, we were lucky if we saw a new outfit from Walmart. Mostly, our clothes came from Salvation Army or Goodwill. The Grove offered so many choices it was overwhelming, and I really couldn't concentrate enough to buy anything. I really hadn't fully grasped my new situation either at that point and was still living as if on a Salvation Army budget. Gradually, over time, I became more comfortable with my new life, and shopping came more naturally. I must admit I do love to shop. I especially love shoes. Shoes are great because no matter what you look like or if you are a little overweight like me, shoes remain the same size and look good. To me, a good shoe makes all the difference in an outfit. Tall boots became an obsession for a bit and then wedges. Wedges are so awesome because you can walk in them, unlike a spiky heel, which is the worst to walk in. Wedges make me feel taller, which I desperately need because I am vertically challenged and need help reaching the top shelf. Wedges became my best friend for a while and helped me reach new heights—and high shelves! Although I always go back to a nice comfy walking slip-on. Clogs are my go-to for the barn and errands, and Skechers are my favorite for exercise.

My hair has gone through the ups and downs with me, too. My hair coming out of the backyard was limp and lifeless, kind of like how I felt. Dragged down by the pressure of life and weighted down with so much dirty garbage of Phillip and Nancy's making. My hair reflected all that I was at the time. Maybe no one noticed, but I did, and it was tough to change and figure out what I wanted my hair to look like. Slowly we went through many changes and styles together, my hair and me. In the backyard, Phillip allowed Nancy to take me out to town, but I always had to color my hair first. I learned not to care what my hair looked like or feel anything for it because it was just a thing that got in the way of my freedom for the day. Later, when I had the choice, I relied on the advice of others because I really didn't know what to do with it.

The media played a role in my decision as well, and I had one style for the press and one style for home. I tried dark, I tried light, and it made me feel like I was two people in one body at times. The more I changed it, the more I figured out what I liked and what I didn't. I eventually experimented with adding bangs, which I thought made me look cute but too young, and then I cut it really short for some reason I can't even remember. I tried highlights and lowlights and finally back to blond and I grew it out long. After all this experimentation with different styles, I like the way it looks now and feel it looks most like how I see myself when I close my eyes and picture myself. That self does not exist, I know, but dreaming you look like a 6'2" supermodel with a mane of long, flowing, golden locks and long, elegant legs, perfect for reaching any shelf in the house and no need to wrap their stirrups when horseback riding, is sometimes what I picture. Hey, a girl can dream.

Clothes have been a similar journey for me. And like my hair, clothes have evolved into what I like to call "My Style." Gone are the days of the coverup from head to toe and gender-neutral clothes. Cover up everything was my theme for some time, and then jeans and T-shirts came into fashion. As a kid, I wore nothing but stretch pants and had a pair in every color imaginable, with my favorite being pink. My style has really changed this past year. I discovered Nordstrom Rack. I walked into the store one day and said, This is a magical land! Filled full of nice designer brands at half the cost of the expensive ones I will not buy because I like a good bargain just like my mom does. Today I would have to say my favorite kinds of clothes are the comfy kind. I love wearing exercise clothes. They are so comfy and cozy and make me feel like I exercise a lot more than I actually do, so that's a bonus! These days I do feel more grown-up than I have ever felt in the past. Almost like these last six years have been my "awkward teen" years that I missed out on and now I'm in the more "I'm comfortable, this is me" zone. Maybe I'm just deluding myself about the grown-up part! I tend to wear more girly clothes now. I found that I really like dresses and patterns. My style tends to be flowy with fitted at the top and more flare at the bottom. My body has changed, too, from exercising at least three days a week with weight training mixed in and still hiking with Rebecca and friends any chance I have.

Who's That Girl on TV?

I had always dreamed of being a writer. My dream came true. For me, writing *A Stolen Life* was very cathartic, and I look back on the experience with awe and wonder that I actually did it. I became an author. *A Stolen Life* was published in 2011. I was asked to do an interview to accompany the release. Nanny Goat gave me several names to choose from for the interview. After meeting Diane Sawyer, I knew she was the one for me. Not only was she kind but she also felt completely normal and not the famous and beautiful Diane Sawyer I knew from the news!

During the interview, Diane was incredibly nice and real with me. I had watched her on TV for years in the backyard and to be face-to-face with her and Chris Cuomo was surreal. I was happy to be interviewed but at the same time quite nervous. It was probably hard to tell, though, because I had had so much practice disguising my anxiety, I don't think anyone really knew. I had shaky hands and sweaty palms. I guess I really had good reason to be nervous. I was kidnapped at eleven, I had been in some loon and his loony-toon's wife's backyard for eighteen years. The only real contact I had was with them and my two daughters. Conversations consisted mostly of lectures about the Bible from Phillip, and now here I was, a real-life book author of my very own book. I think my nerves were totally justified.

I was worried about someone finding out I was nervous. Why did that make me nervous? Maybe because I was afraid they would think I didn't want to do the interview. Or maybe they would think I couldn't handle it. I can handle anything. (I lie to myself quite often, I've noticed.) The line "Fake it till you make it" was playing over and over in my mind. Not sure where I heard that, but it was one of those phrases that has always stuck with me. Even in the backyard. Fake that smile till you live that smile. That day I definitely didn't want anyone to know, and so I just did it. I just tried to act like I belonged on that interview set and that it was just an ordinary day for me. La-tee-da. They really did make it as comfortable as possible. Nanny Goat made sure of that. Only a couple of cameras and only essential staff on set. My mom was there and was a calming influence on me as well. Rebecca, my constant supporter and cheer team rolled into one, was also on set. I received the red carpet treatment with hair and makeup done professionally. I had brought my own outfit from home, which I had picked out myself. The day was bright and sunny, and I felt like I was going to throw up.

The day went by very fast and before you knew it, we were done and off to dinner. Diane ordered everything from the menu to try and even all the desserts to share. I have always had a sweet tooth, so that to me was an excellent way to end what turned out to be a fabulous day. And best yet, nobody knew I was nervous. Sometimes looking back, I wonder what if I had let my real feelings through. The interview had been very open and honest. What if I had just told someone "Hey, I'm a bit nervous"? Would that have been so bad? Would the world end if I showed vulnerability? Probably not. Growth comes with time, and slowly I have learned I do not have to always be alert, on guard, and un-sharing of my feelings. Tough to learn, but it comes with rewards. Like better relationships with the ones you love.

Now, years later, when I watch the Diane Sawyer interview I get this strange feeling of being detached from it in a way. Almost like that wasn't me in the story, yet I know it was. One time Rebecca and I watched it together while preparing for an upcoming presentation, and as I looked up at her at one point, she was crying and I was, too. Even though she knew my whole story and I had lived, it wasn't until that moment that it just all hit me and apparently her, too. We were both kind of like, Wow, did that happen to you? Yep, every moment of it was me in that interview and I had lived to tell the tale. "How incredible," we both said aloud. I have always felt so normal and average in every way. Even after the interview, I still felt not like a big celeb but the same shy person I have always been.

In 2011, I formed the JAYC Foundation, which stands for Just Ask Yourself to Care! I wanted to have a lasting legacy and to give back all that I could. But how? I saw the benefits firsthand of the work Rebecca and her team did for us as a whole family, and I wanted that for every family that was going through trauma in their lives. During the creation process, I didn't want the foundation to be named after me. I feel like a lot of foundations bear the name of someone that had not come back, and I wanted my foundation to be different. I was very much alive. So I decided to use part of my name, JAYC, and I wanted each letter to be part of a greater message. You are probably thinking, Hey, how did you come up with that way cool acronym? Well, I had help. Rebecca, Jane, her cotherapist, and I thought about what the letters of JAYC could stand for. The result is something I think has a clear and positive message: Just Ask Yourself to Care!

Sometimes I travel for the foundation and give presentations about what we do, and we use the interview to introduce me to those who haven't heard my story. On most of these trips, seeing the interview feels like watching someone else live those moments. But after that happened with Rebecca, something clicked, and I have never been able to watch it without a sense of awe for myself for surviving such a horrible situation. I viewed myself as a person for once. An incredible person that survived against the odds. That feels funny to say about myself, but in that moment I truly gave myself a pat on the back.

After one presentation, an older gentleman came up to me and said, "You could have been a Marine." I shook his hand and asked why, and he said, "Because Marines persevere against incredible odds and survive no matter what they have to do and, that, young lady, is what you did." I smiled and thanked him for his kind words. I think we forget how brave we all are sometimes, and it can be hard to pat yourself on the back. Survival is important, but what I think is important is the ability to forgive, love, and help yourself through the tough patches of your life.

Before the interview the media was in a frenzy wanting a piece of me and my kids, too. It felt like I was the person in a line from that Britney Spears song saying "You want a piece of me." While on a visit at Nanny Goat's house, I released a video pleading for privacy. My mom released a press release stating the same and that we would release what we wanted in our own time. I stayed inside our house for the first week until the press died down, and at times it felt like being a prisoner in the backyard all over again! The girls continued with their normal routine. They had just started school and were still under the watchful eye of key school administrators helping us out with safety. The media was popping up, but I didn't want to take that new freedom from them. I felt it was important that I maintain a low profile because I didn't want to be stopped in the street and asked, "Hey, are you that girl?"

The paparazzi eventually died down, and I felt more at ease coming and going. The neighborhood that we were in at the time was wonderful; even though neighbors didn't know we were there, they all helped in their own way. The chief of police, who had become a very good friend, said he must have gotten a dozen calls from neighbors complaining about the strange cars and people in the neighborhood, which helped us out a lot. Sometimes you don't even know you are doing someone a kindness or how much you are impacting someone's life.

Take me, for instance. I never would have thought I could impact someone's life, but I received so many positive letters after the interview and release of my book, *A Stolen Life*. I was taken completely by surprise and humbled. I even received a letter from Alyssa Milano and one of my favorite authors, Danielle Steel! Who would have ever thought little ol' Jaycee Dugard would have the chance to become a . . . a what? Not a star, but somebody who had written her own book, and that book was something that others were learning valuable lessons from. I never would have imagined that people across the world would benefit from my writings. A book filled with the accounts of my life and the lives of my daughters as prisoners in the backyard and how I tried to make it the best I could so that they could grow up the best that they could in dire circumstances.

"SMILE"

A grungy-looking man in dirty clothes stands on the side of the road. He's holding up a bright yellow sign with bold, black letters that read **"SMILE."**

A reminder to smile? How odd, I thought to myself. Do I really need a reminder? Do people really need a reminder to smile? I guess I do sometimes. I feel like the queen of smiling most days, and yet I need to be reminded at times, too. That day, seeing that sign being held up made me remember to be present in the moment. In that moment I was free and, best of all, I was driving all by myself!

I was just running errands. Doing something mundane like grocery shopping, dropping off a package at the post office, picking up some milk, or perhaps grabbing a Starbucks iced caramel macchiato. I remember spotting that sign while waiting for a light to turn green. At first I didn't smile. Actually, his sign made me kind of sad. I thought, Jeez, do we really need someone on the side of the road telling us to smile? Is the world so crazy all joy has left us? Are we all just going about the motions of our day? Are people so numb they can't even enjoy simple things? I sure hoped not. I know, believe me, sometimes you just don't feel like smiling. But then in that second I remembered all the reasons I had to smile. One of the best ones was exactly what I was doing in that moment—driving! Driving a car down a street, doing something people do every single day without even thinking about it. Something I never really thought I would be able or even allowed to do.

There are so many reasons I love being able to drive. It would be nearly impossible to list them all. For me, the absolute best part of driving is singing in the car. I hear the first few notes of "Take On Me" by A-ha and before you know it, my mouth is moving to the music. I'm one of those singers that hums a few bars and sings only the parts I know. I know I'm singing off-key with lead singer Morten Harket, but I can hit those high notes just like him! It doesn't matter what I sound like in the car. Well. I must admit sometimes it does matter what I sound like just a little bit. When it matters is when I try to sing with the girls in the car. It doesn't go so well because I know I really can't sing. If I could pick one person to sing like it would be Florence Welch from Florence and the Machine. Her voice sounds so rich and intense and perfect! The other day when I was belting it out, I looked over at my oldest daughter, who was laughing into her jacket. She is one of those people who knows all the lyrics to a song she hears only once! I'd love to be like that, but alas, I am tone deaf.

Oh well, at least my dog doesn't mind. Belt it out I say! He hasn't howled yet.

I was so nervous to learn how to drive. My hands were sweating and I was giddy like I couldn't stop grinning. I had to totally defy that part of me that had been conditioned never to touch a steering wheel. I can tell you I dreamed about it a million times.

One of the very first things I learned to do when I was recovered was learn to drive with some gentle prodding from my mom and sister. And, lo and behold, I became a race car driver! Just kidding! Sitting in my mom's car and listening as the gears and buttons were explained to me, that's the moment I truly started to feel like an adult. Before then I felt very young and unsure of myself. Even though I was already a mom, I think the events in your life shape you, and although I have had my share of unsavory events, I didn't have those milestones that happen as you grow up.

Sitting in that car I felt like I was going to get in trouble. Like someone was going to yell and shout, "Get out of the car, idiot! You can't possibly think you can drive!" But I told myself, Phillip and Nancy no longer had a chokehold on my life. I could do it if I wanted. I wanted to drive! I could and I would.

Off we went for my first driving lesson. I learned on a curvy hill road. It was pretty private, and I didn't have to pass a lot of cars. Good thing, because I am not sure I even stayed on my side of the road. Not sure what I would have done if someone had come down the hill at the same time I was going up. I learned later that it's very intimidating passing cars for the first time. It got easier the more practice I got. That first day, I remember thinking, Yikes, I am actually driving my first car! I focused on everything my sister was saying and put that nagging voice out of my head. I have to give my sister credit for not having a panic attack. I am sure I scared her a few times around some curves. She was a very patient teacher. I thought a few times how strange it was that my little sister was teaching me to drive. After all, I hadn't seen her since she was a small baby. And now here she was teaching her big sister how to drive.

The day I actually took my driver's test was dreamlike. My mom drove me to the DMV. (Again the nauseating nerves. Would they ever leave me alone?) I couldn't string together a whole sentence the entire way there. The instructor asked if I was ready, and I must have said yes or maybe I just smiled and nodded. Suddenly I was in the car checking my mirrors and pulling out into the road. He asked me to do my hand signals out the window. I totally botched them, not exactly sure which was which. But I guess I must have done okay, or maybe he just felt really sorry for me. I pulled back into the DMV parking lot and parked a little crooked and at least a foot from the curb. The instructor said, Congratulations! You passed, Miss Dugard! I jumped out and went to hug my mom with a big grin on my face. My mom was laughing; she had noticed the parking job. Oh, well, I passed! I got my license!

On the car ride home, I was calling and texting everyone I knew. My mother had to drive because I was too excited to do it myself. My aunt Tina was teaching her class but picked up and was super excited for me. My sister sent me happy-face emojis. When I called Rebecca, she picked up in a whisper, which was strange. I told her I passed! I must have really shouted loud because I could hear someone ask her on the other end, Is that your daughter? Rebecca explained to me she was at her uncle Senator Matthias's funeral reception in Washington and that she was in a little box of a room called the "cell phone room." There were a few senators having their own conversations. She told me they looked irritated by her interruption and not impressed when she apologized and tried to explain who I was. I guess I had never really thought about that before. How do you explain me to any-one? I mean, even I find my own story hard to believe. Like I have said a million times, who gets taken by a deranged couple and comes back eighteen years later with two beautiful children? Doesn't sound real even to me.

Driving has taken a little getting used to. At times that insecure voice creeps in, and I battle it back with my mental nunchackus. I have learned a trick that works 80 percent of the time—just do it! Nike was right! All those clichés have proven to be right. "Fake it till you make it." "One step at a time." "Get 'er done." All the jargon words people live by, but guess what? They really work!

My best friend, Jessie, comes up for visits whenever she can. She picks the oddest hours to fly. Inevitably, it would be in the dead of night. I used to dread the drive. What would happen if I had an accident? Or worse yet, if my car broke down or if I got lost in some scary part of town? The first time she asked me to pick her up at night, I was excited to see my friend, but night driving is so different from day driving. The headlights are so bright and make it hard to see. That kind of motivation, though, has helped me to become a pretty proficient driver with lots of airport runs under my belt. Those drives to and from the airport have been the best practice I could ever get. I have even found out it's a good time to think about things.

At first I mostly stayed in the slow lane. Although I quickly discovered that lane was ruled by trucks. I hated changing lanes. I watched how other people drove, which was helpful to me. I have been told I'm a visual learner. That made really good sense to me. Because anything I do I must observe it first. Everything from writing checks for the first time to learning to canter on my horse was done by me watching someone. If I see it, I can do it. I learn an awful lot watching YouTube videos.

I drove with my two hands on the wheel for quite awhile. Jerky stops were my MO. As I became more comfortable, my hand position changed to a more relaxed, natural position. At times I still find my two hands on the wheel, even today. I think my age and common sense have helped to make me a pretty safe driver. I mean, I like to think I did not go through all this to get in a car accident. My car is more than just a vehicle of transportation. It is a symbol to smile. It takes me anywhere I need or want to go. It's a strange feeling at times. Even now, being free and able to go where I want surprises me a little bit. I wonder if the feeling of surprise ever truly disappears.

I remember the first time I got pulled over. I was coming back from a friend's house late one night. Cars were slowing down on the road, and we were wondering what was going on. We saw there was a police checkpoint up along the highway. The sign said DUI Checkpoint. Everybody had to show their license to an officer when they passed a certain point in the roadblock. Even though it was dark, there were powerful floodlights everywhere.

The lights blinded me as I pulled up. When it was my turn, I pulled up and held my license out. The officer asked me some questions. Do you live here, and where are you headed? I said I lived close and was headed home. He said, Why do you have a different address on your license? And I said for privacy reasons. Instead of waving us through, he told me to pull over to the side parking lot and wait there. I was really nervous. I was afraid I had done something wrong. There were a few other cars waiting, too, but I felt singled out. Like there was something else going on besides just a DUI checkpoint. Another officer came over, and I gave him my name and explained my circumstances, the reason why I chose to have a different address on my license. I told him in a shaky voice that must have been ringing bells in his head that something was wrong. But I couldn't help myself. It was the first time I had been pulled over, and I didn't know how to react. Or what was going on, for that matter. I told him he could call the chief of police for the county and that he could verify it with him. The chief had been a friend since the beginning of us moving into the neighborhood. The officer said to wait here in the car and he would check it out. I was kind of shaky but told myself everything was okay and I hadn't done anything to be in trouble for. It wasn't like being in the backyard. I had no reason to hide my identity from the police. Within a few minutes, the officer came back and started apologizing profusely. He told me we could be on our way. I was so relieved. I pulled out and forgot to buckle my seat belt, I was so anxious.

Later, I really wanted to be mad. I didn't like the feelings that were popping up. Why was I put through that? Was it really just a DUI check? Or something more? Clearly, I had not been drinking. Thinking about it later as I lay awake in bed, I really felt something else was going on. It felt like they were actually looking for someone.

The next day as I read in the paper about a missing person in the area, my suspicions were verified. Even though it was tough to go through that the night before, I realized I was happy—happy they saw something that didn't look right to them and pulled me over to check it out. Even though I had not been who they were looking for, they were doing their job. They left no stone unturned.

The scariest thing happened on my birthday while I was driving my car. It was my thirty-third birthday, and my best friend, Jessie, had flown up for it. I didn't want to do anything special. Just have a relaxing day. As I picked her up at the airport and pulled out onto the highway—SMACK! A bird had flown directly into my windshield and went *splat!* It actually made that sound. OMG! I remember shouting, and Jessie echoed my sentiment. I didn't know what to do. It was so stressful, I started to giggle. Sometimes I giggle or laugh at the most inappropriate moments, and this was one of them. Luckily, my friend didn't think I was a complete loon because she started laughing, too! *Splat!* OMG! Another one? What is happening? This is my birthday! How could two birds hit my car one after another! On my birthday! Don't they know this is a special day? I guess they didn't get the memo. Jessie said I should put the windshield wipers on. Well, you can imagine what that did. Smeared the poor birds, or what was left of them, all over the windshield. I could hardly see out now. I pulled into a gas station and we went to work getting the guts off. Those birds must have been traveling fast because I had just started to pick up speed.

At the gas station we were still running high on emotion with the evidence of tears running down our faces. I had never hit anything before, and it was traumatic. Laughing about it helped relieve the pressure of the situation. This was not how I pictured my birthday going. I felt so bad for killing the birds, but Jessie reminded me that the birds did fly into my windshield and there was nobody to blame. I drove us home. She turned up the radio and we sang songs all the way home. She is just as bad a singer as I am, so together I'm sure we sounded great!

Cold Soup?

For many years of my captive life, food came in a bag. Sometimes with those famous golden arches and sometimes with a crown. It got boring after a while, but it was what I knew and later what my daughters knew as food for most of their lives.

Before Phillip's mother became demented, she would cook meals on Sundays. It was a real treat for us when Phillip or Nancy would bring homemade chili beans or some kind of homemade dinner to the back for us. Those were luxuries we normally did not have.

When we were first recovered in 2009, we were introduced to Rebecca's husband, Charles. He had been a professional chef for many years and was now helping out with food prep at their Transitioning Families program.

In those days after recovery, food choices were not something

I was used to making unless it involved telling someone what I wanted from the drive-thru. So when we were brought to a house that first month of transition and Chef Charles asked what kinds of food I would like stocked in the house, I had no idea what to say, so I just said, "The basics, please."

The next day as I rummaged through our stocked refrigerator looking for some tasty morsel to munch on, I came across the peanut butter—peanut butter in the fridge? Weird! My peanut butter, even as a little girl, was Skippy and lived in the cabinet. This one was an organic kind and had a funny layer of oil on the top. I was embarrassed to ask, but sometimes it's better to ask those you trust than find out from strangers, so I asked why the peanut butter looked like it did. Was it spoiled? No, the reply was, that's just how some organic peanut butter is. You have to mix it because the oil separates. However weird and new this new peanut butter was, it was tasty and went great with the organic strawberry jelly. "Organic" was not in our vocabulary yet. Yes, we knew what it was from hearing about the new fad on TV, but we had been lucky to just get plain fresh fruit and veggies whether they were organic or not.

Another culinary discovery came in the form of something I had not encountered before. We had been invited to a very sacred place called the Maple Ring. The history of the place goes back generations, and I was told that the local Indian tribes would use the trees as burial spots for their food when they needed to store it. Legend has it that all the maple trees sprang up from the one in the middle and they all lean toward their mother and form a circle around her. This story kind of reminds me of me and how I just wanted to be near my mom all those years Phillip and

Nancy kept me prisoner. The story also says that other trees were planted in the area, but they always grow away from this mother tree and her maple offspring.

That day we felt honored to be able to share the day together in such a beautiful place. Chef Charles had prepared us a family picnic lunch complete with fun napkins with turkeys on them and straws made out of paper. Our first course was soup. But not just ordinary soup. Chef Charles had prepared us something new that day.

As I prepared to sample this soup, my daughters blurted out, "Hey, this soup is cold!" Chef Charles said it was supposed to be. It's cold on purpose? What trickery is this? I thought. COLD SOUP! After the initial shock wore off and we knew it was cold on purpose, it was easier to taste again. I thought it would be gross, but whatever Chef Charles makes must at least be tried once. At first, when it hit my mouth it felt wrong, like when you taste cold mashed potatoes, but then all the flavors come rushing at you, and I found myself with another spoonful ready for the hatch. It really was quite an experience and memorable. I learned that some kinds of cold soup are called gazpacho. Chef Charles made this one from tomatoes, shallots, and slivers of avocado.

Also served were delicate tea sandwiches to go with our soup and a fluffy salad made with a type of lettuce called frisée. The food got us all talking, and it was nice because we had been talking in therapy about some tough topics and the break was much needed.

Throughout our time at the Transitioning Families program, my daughters and I learned from Chef Charles how to prepare tasty meals. Much to Chef Charles's dismay, none of his lessons have stuck with me, and I will not be the next Top Chef! This, however, was one aspect of the program I loved the most, besides working with the horses. And to this day, the families we support to come to the JAYC Foundation for reunification all take away a special culinary moment with each other.

Food is such a versatile thing. Have you ever really thought about how important food is to all of us? I have. It's something that we all have in common. It brings people together from everywhere around the world and even the toughest days seem like a walk in the park because you are eating the most delicious pasta primavera you have ever eaten in your life! Food can be good, bad, ugly, beautiful, delicate, heavy, and every color of the rainbow. I think food plays an important role in all our lives, and we can always count on it to be the subject of conversation when nothing else comes to mind.

I have found it an especially useful topic when the not so great topic of politics comes up. I used to think I wasn't smart enough to talk politics with people. Phillip always made me think my opinions were not good enough, so I learned to keep my opinion to myself. Relearning that it's okay to have an opinion has taken time. It's not an overnight process to all of a sudden be comfortable talking about my thoughts and feelings, but I have become more comfortable with receiving the negative and positive aspects of conversations. Most of the time I can really see both sides of an opinion or argument a candidate makes. I hate it when people talk in absolutes, though. Because really, is anything in life absolute? Gosh, I really can't imagine having Donald Trump as a president. All I can see and hear when he talks is "You're fired" from his show *The Apprentice*. I feel like the whole country is turning into one big reality show. Really, that's what the debates have turned into: TV ratings. And it's all coming down to who is the most entertaining. At times I find myself just laughing at the absurdity of it all. In my world, it's all good, though. I try to see the good in just about everything. It's not an easy thing, but I like the challenge! Food conversation always trumps politics in my book.

It was not hard to instill a love of fruits and veggies into my kids. In fact, they are both vegetarians and they love to cook, something that my mom (their grandma), who is a fabulous cook, and Chef Charles instilled in them. It works for me because I like to be cooked for!

I've learned a lot from Chef Charles throughout the years, and he has also been a very good friend to me and my family. He always encourages me to try new foods, so in the spirit of trying new things, which is very important to me because life in the backyard was so boring, I tried sea bass for the first time. I've never been a big fan of fish and usually stay away from it, but the sea bass was actually delicious. It was delicate and didn't have a fishy taste at all. Since then I have also tried swordfish, salmon, ceviche, and tuna. I really liked the sea bass the best, though.

I think it's always good to try new things unless it's scallops, oysters, or snails! I have to draw the line at snails and slimy things. I also cannot stand the taste of cilantro. I have tried my hardest to like it because one of my favorite kinds of food is Mexican, but the taste of cilantro always ruins it for me. Chef Charles tries to be sneaky sometimes and tell me it's only parsley, but you can't fool me: my tastebuds always know!

I've always been one to follow what I think of as rules. Chef

Charles had a rule about no minis in his garden. He dearly loved his garden, and whenever Rebecca would let the miniature horses out to graze, he would always shout, "Keep those guys out of my garden!"

At first I saw Charles as the "guy in charge" and didn't want to break his rules. But as I got to know him better, I realized he wasn't like other men that had been in my life. He was encouraging, kind, and had a wry sense of humor that brought out my sarcastic side. And before I knew it, I was not even listening to his so-called rules anymore. He just made them up anyway.

One of his rules was "No clients riding in the arena." Before my family came along, Rebecca would just do on-the-ground horse exercises with her clients. She knew me and my mom needed something more, though, so one day, much to Chef Charles's dismay, she had me sit on Velcro blindfolded while my mom took the lead rope and lead us around the arena. Mom led the way and kept me safe at the same time. It was a beautiful moment for me and my mom for building trust in our relationship.

Another time that I broke the "rules," Chef Charles actually taught me how. I was looking for some hutches for my daughter's baby chicks she had rescued. My daughter loves animals as much as I do and didn't want to see these sweet babies get hurt. So she brought them home, and we made a coop together for them.

Chef Charles said he knew where I could get some for-free hutches for them. I thought, Free sounds good. But where? He took us to the back of a grocery store where they had crates and boxes from the food. He said the crates would make excellent hutches. I felt like there was some law against just taking the crates, but he said it was okay to take them. I felt like we were stealing from the grocery store. Was this an irrational fear? Yes, probably, but I was just used to doing things differently. It felt freeing in a way, though, and I didn't really think I was hurting the grocery store or anyone for that matter. Chef Charles seemed confident that it was okay, and for the first time I broke what I thought was a rule. I stole the crates for the chickens! I felt kind of guilty. But it also felt kind of good, too. I learned to be more flexible that day. Some rules are meant to be broken . . . well, maybe a little.

A Dream Is a Wish Your Heart Makes . . . When You're Missing

I had never had a housewarming party before. In fact, I had never owned my own home before either. I have been lucky in my new life to have experienced both.

The day was bright and clear with no chance of rain in the forecast. Very lucky for us because before that day, we had been getting rain every day. This day was clear and reflected my feelings. We had just moved in a few days before, and it felt so good and comfortable. Almost like an old shoe that fits just right the first time you put it on. This house felt like that. We decided to keep our cats in for the first month or so to get them used to their new home. Bull just loved running the hills and smelling all the new smells. Best of all, I never really have to pick up his poops anymore because he always goes where no one can see him in the bushes. He's shy like that.

The day of the housewarming party all our new friends and family gathered to celebrate us moving in. I had no idea they had a big surprise for me that day, one that I would cherish forever.

When everyone arrived, we all gathered on the deck of our new house. One by one they read special cards with clues about my surprise. Jane had written them especially for the occasion.

Jane read the first clue:

"Clue number one. Once upon a time there was an eleven-year-old girl who went missing."

The card went on to say:

Stop the presses! This is not a story about a little girl who went missing; it's a story about a lovely young woman who reentered the real world. On August 26th, 2009, the anniversary of Women's Suffrage Day, the young woman celebrated the first day of the rest of her life. While this young woman grew up in captivity, she had many dreams that kept her going. Today we will revisit how, with the help of Team Jaycee, family, and friends, some of her dreams have come true. This is a treasure hunt, Jaycee. The prize is a housewarming gift from your team. Find the next clue #2 and make sure it is read aloud.

I found clue number two. One of my new friends read it aloud:

"One of the dreams of the young woman was to have friends and for her daughters to have friends. They came to a house on Buena Vista where all kinds of people were in and out. Oh my! How overwhelming! To name but a few, there was Rebecca and Jane, Liz and Suni, Cheryl, Harla, and Trish, and on and on. The list would grow and grow: Charles, Theo, Mark, Bill, and

Pat, Nick, Mike, Ana, Janet, Michael, Sean, Dale, Margie, Jack, and even extends to the East Coast with Marsha and Lanae. And don't forget those four-legged friends: Fressia, Velcro, Skye, and Stella. Early in this chaos, you met a man named Todd. He would be a friend for a long time to come. To the beach, helping move . . . need help? Call Todd. In fact, find Todd now because he has your next clue."

Todd read clue number three next:

"You moved to Wood Valley up the hill and hung out for weeks. You wanted your kids to be healthy, so they saw physicians and dentists. The hermit crabs joined you and so did the bird. However, the four kittens you rescued had to stay in foster homes. When you and the girls needed new clothes, a friend took you shopping. And others brought you a brand-new telescope so you could look more closely at the stars and continue to have your dreams. Find clue number four."

I guessed it was with Liz and I was right.

She read clue number four (by this time I was really excited and very emotional).

Clue number four read:

Chief Sackett was good at keeping an eye on you—what a great guy! Most of the time you didn't even know he was driving by. And, lo and behold, your first driving instructor was none other than your tall little sister Shayna! But you started to get restless and needed money to rent a house—so the next step was to plan pictures for the press, hoping they'd be satisfied for a while. Tina made you and your mother beautiful, and you graced the cover of People *magazine. Now, this didn't work out as well as it might* jaycee dugard

because you were missing an important member of your team. Enter Nancy Seltzer also known as Nanny Goat! Find Nanny Goat for the next clue.

Nanny Goat read clue number five:

"You rented a house and moved in November 2009. Finally, you were able to be reunited with those four kittens you had in the backyard. They were bigger now but so happy to be in their new home with you. You snuck in the back door of the DMV before hours and got your driver's license, and I was able to fulfill your wish of transportation. With the help of an anonymous donor, you were blessed with a brand-new car! Find clue number six."

The clue read:

Month after month went by; your little sister left for school. You ran your first 10K at Hit the Road Jack with your own personal cop! The girls were given a patchwork of education help with tutors and home teachers, but you really wanted them to get a formal official education. See if your aunt Tina has a clue to what happened next.

My aunt Tina read the next one:

"Clue number seven."

"You knew your girls were smart, but you didn't want anything to stand in the way of them having choices about college and their future. You have always felt education is important and you knew the choices for your girls would be another dream come

— 46 —

true. Your girls are now enrolled in public school. Find clue number eight."

I read clue number eight.

"Okay, I get it! Life is hard out here, but with help I'm getting there. I'm working on my book, which is being edited as we speak. I was able to get the papers for the JAYC Foundation nonprofit. Dale helped me hold the state accountable for their mistakes, and now I'm off to find a place of my own to live. But I need help—it has to have room for my girls, my cats, my new pal Bull, and a special place for my mom. Mom—what a great word—in fact, she has the next clue."

My mom read clue number nine.

"We looked and looked at one house after another. Some were too big and some were too small. Some smelled funny and some needed too much work. You wanted room for horses, so we looked at some with barns. I have never given up hope that you would be found—and now in a new part of California we have new friends and a new home. And here we are—welcome home, kid."

That put me over the edge as she gave me a big hug and I let the tears stream down my face. Thinking, Gosh, I must be the luckiest person alive right now to have so many people that love me. And it wasn't over yet—I still had that big surprise to find!

Another friend read clue number nine:

"There is so much more to this story, more than any of us will ever know. It has become the story of how a brave young mother and her two young daughters were reunited with a grieving mother, aunt, and sister. This new, larger family has a long road ahead, but with the help of a team of friends and the support of each other, they will persevere. A new home, wonderful pets, plans for a foundation to help others. But wait! One more thing: go see Rebecca for your last clue."

Rebecca read the last clue that she wrote herself:

"On the twenty-seventh of August the phone rang at six a.m. It was NCMEC [National Center for Missing and Exploited Children] calling. They had an interesting case for me to consider. It involved the discovery of a missing girl who now had two children, a mother, a sister, an aunt, and a boatload of media freaks. I didn't know what I was getting myself into. Team Jaycee kicked into gear. We found a house for you and stocked the refrigerator with food unfamiliar to you, and the rest is history. Recently I learned that it was not our renowned competence that brought you to us. Rather, you believed that an old woman psychologist had a ranch where you could teach your daughters to ride horses. Welcome to my humble abode. The animals quickly became an important part of the team. From the moment Stella gobbled up poison, to your mad dash to the hospital with Bull, it has been clear that animals are never far from your heart.

"However, as we look around this incredible place, there seems to be something missing. But never fear, the team is here! We reached out to your friends and searched high and low for the perfect pinecone. The prettiest of all is a pinecone that resembles a flower. It is called a wood rose. We brought one for you today— Jaycee, meet Woodrose."

By this time, we were all gathered at the barn as she read the last paragraph of the clue. I have my eyes closed. When I open them, Margie is there in front of me walking up with the most gorgeous horse I had ever seen. My jaw literally dropped (I really thought that only happened in movies). Love at first sight. I was so stunned I didn't know what to say. She handed me the reins, and I just threw my arms around him. What are the odds they found this horse for me with a name like Woodrose, which is a type of pinecone? For one thing, he is a boy horse, and it just struck me as such a girly name. And second, I have always had this connection with pinecones since I was taken at age eleven. It was the last thing I touched.

My very own horse. Wow! I couldn't believe all my friends and family got together and bought me my very own first horse. A beautiful Western saddle, too, and reins. I led him into the arena where I got on him for a ride for the first time. Margie led me around, and I remember waving like some kind of queen on her horse. I felt so special and loved. After me, my daughters each took a turn on him, too. I don't remember much more of that day. I was so overcome with emotion. Oh yeah, I do remember the delicious chocolate cake shaped like a pinecone that a friend had made special for the occasion. It was the first pinecone cake I had ever had, and it was yummy. It was almost like a flourless chocolate cake, and it was in the shape of a pinecone, and she had decorated it to look like one, too. It was incredible. That whole day was incredible.

Woodrose soon acquired the nickname of Cowboy. He was previously owned by a cowboy. Margie is a horse trainer and was the one who found him for the team to give to me. She took him to her place for a couple weeks and worked with him until the big day came to bring him to me. She started to call him Cowboy during those days, and it just felt right when she did. I learned that I was the ninth owner of Woodrose. I was stunned to learn that because he seemed like such a nice horse. Why would he have so many previous owners? He is a Haflinger and some say the jokesters of the horse world. I can see that in him sometimes. He does seem to like having fun but not in a harmful way. He will pull to eat grass, but I've learned to just be clear about what we are doing, and he usually gets the hint. I have had so many fun rides on him throughout the years, and Margie has taught me a lot about horses. I know I will be his last owner. He will never again have another.

When I was a kid I didn't think about the building blocks of relationships. I knew my mom loved me and my family, and it wasn't really something I needed to work at. As a grown-up, I know people in the real world don't just automatically love you or even like you. You have to work on yourself and like yourself, I think, in order for others to like you. Animals are different. Well, I like to think they are different and they all love me no matter what. I know my dog does. Every time he sees me, I know he is so happy. It shows in every aspect of his body language. My cats love me, too. They have a different way of showing love, and sometimes I think they just like me because I feed them. When my cat Zelda seeks me out for a cuddle, I admit my mind goes to Hey, you're just looking for a warm spot. But then I think there are a million warm spots for her in this house, and she chose me. I think that means something. Horses are different. I expected to feel a connection right away with my new horse. Although he was nice and had nice manners and didn't seem to mind me, I didn't get that feeling of love that I obviously felt for him already. Which made me question myself. Do I love you? How can I? I just met you, for gosh sake. Why do I go instantly to love? The real question I should have been asking myself was, Who are you? What do you like and dislike? Can we be friends? The answers to these questions came slowly, and I learned I didn't have to be loved instantly by my horse, because I was getting something so much better than love: I was learning how to build a relationship with my horse.

Getting to know him was a little frustrating because I wanted instant gratification. And he just would not deliver. I groomed him three times a week and learned every curve and groove of his body. I picked the eye buggers from his eyes and learned to clean the dreaded sheath. Nasty job but just a part of owning a boy horse, ladies. During this time, I was still afraid of so many things about riding and really unsure of myself. Rebecca was helping me with my confidence, and we did a lot of ground work together. She taught me how to "join up" with my horse, which required us both to trust each other and for him to acknowledge I was in charge of our relationship. The work I was doing on the ground translated into my riding lessons with Margie, too.

My most mad moment with Cowboy came early in our journey. Rebecca, Charles, and I decided to take our horses for a walk. Just a walk: we thought no big deal. Well, one of the horses spooked at something and Rebecca got a kick to her hand and was in excruciating pain. I wanted to run to her right away, but I was tethered with a big responsibility. Freesia took off running, which made Velcro want to run. Luckily, Charles had a good hold on her. I had a hold of Cowboy, but he was getting really prancy standing in place. I felt torn between wanting to go to Rebecca to see if she was okay and getting the horses back to the barn.

Charles started out with Velcro to go collect Freesia, who really hadn't gone that far. Horses are herd animals and like to stay together. So as he got her and started walking back to the barn, I went over to Rebecca. I was shaking pretty badly at that point. Seeing her in so much pain was hard. She was about ready to pass out. I was scared. Horses do pick up what you are feeling, and even though I had a hold on my lead rope, Cowboy felt a million miles away in his brain. He kept looking in the direction of the barn and the other horses. He wanted to be with them and not me. I know it's dumb, but I kind of took that personally. Why wasn't he okay just being with me? Didn't he know I wouldn't let anything happen to him? Apparently not, because I could feel his focus was not on me. I told Rebecca that I would take him back to the barn and come back for her as soon as I could. I was scared to go back all by myself. It was just him and me out on the trail. It was a narrow trail, too, with a hill on one side and a bit of a drop on the other. He was practically dragging me at one point. We had no trust in our relationship yet.

I didn't realize then but I know now that it takes time to build that kind of relationship with your horse. In his haste to move forward more, he went up the side of the hill, which had me on my knees from the sudden change in terrain. I was not letting go. My hands were hurting from the rope burn he was giving me and it was hard not to be mad. In fact, I was mad! I was finally mad at my horse for being such a doofus and hurting me! Why didn't he trust me more? As I'm on my knees with blood coming out of a cut, I wanted to give up and just let him go. Give up and go back to my friend who was hurting, but I couldn't do it. I looked up at him and shouted, "Hey! Stop that and get down here!" Maybe

Me, Nanny Goat, and Rebecca.

Me on my first horse.

*Sitting on my new horse
for the first time.*

it was the sound of my voice or maybe he just remembered I was there, but he took a few steps down from the hill, and I picked myself up. He started to want to pull again, and as he took the first of what was to become I'm sure his many steps, I just planted my feet and stood my ground. "No!" I said. This made Cowboy come to a sudden stop. He was surprised at our lack of motion and looked at me for what I realized was the first time since the whole ordeal started. For the first time I really had his attention, not the horses he could hear whinnying in the distance. We looked at each other and I said to him, "It's okay, boy, we are okay," and I patted his nose. I knew I needed to get my emotions under control so I could get back to the barn unharmed and go back and help my friend. I took a deep breath, and he did, too. I decided I needed something to occupy my thoughts for a while so I started to sing "Twinkle, Twinkle, Little Star" over and over again.

As we marched forward together, the mad went away and I started to just talk to him and tell him what we were doing and that we would be back with his friends soon and then I could help my friend. I realized he was just scared. I think after that he trusted me a lot more. We made it back to the barn, and I raced back to help Rebecca. Charles took her to the hospital for her hand, which turned out to have a fracture. Very scary moments, but I learned that even in chaos you have the ability to make it what you want if you just sing your trouble away! Twinkle, twinkle, little star . . . how I wonder where you are.

Just Sing!

I love music! All kinds of music from Lady Gaga to Garth Brooks. But the music of the '80s holds my heart. From pop to rock, I love it all. I think it's because it's what I grew up on. My mom would play it in the car as she drove down the freeways of SoCal cooling my French fries out the window so I could eat them.

When I was captive in the backyard, Phillip gave me an old stereo that he said he found in a secondhand shop. It came with two speakers. He said I could play it as long as I kept the volume low, and if he ever heard it from outside, he would take it away. He would use this kind of manipulation all the time to get what he wanted. He said he would hook up the speakers for me when he had time. As days passed without him "having time," I got frustrated and figured out how to connect the speakers myself. I was so excited when I heard that first bit of static! After searching and searching for a station, I finally found one, and I will always remember the first song I heard on that radio. Actually, I had never really heard music like this before. It had been four years since I heard music and it had changed. The song was "Waterfalls," by TLC. Its blend of lyrics and rap was completely new to me, and I sat there captivated. It was catchy. After I heard it the first time, I would catch myself singing it to myself during the day.

> *Don't go chasing waterfalls,*
> *Please stick to the rivers and the lakes that you're used to*

I loved that radio. Somehow it made me feel connected to the world again after so many years apart. A, my first daughter, was just a baby then. I would hold her and dance us around our tiny cramped room to the music. At night when she would wake up, I would turn it down real low and rock her back to sleep. All these years later I still think about that song by TLC and still find myself at times humming it.

"Puppy Love"

My aunt Tina had the cutest boxer named Crash. I loved his goofy personality and the incredible loyalty he showed to my aunt. Tina had gotten Crash in 2009, a few months before I was recovered. Crash was a rescue. He got the name Crash because he had been hit by a car and nearly died. His previous owner did not want to pay to save his life and gave him up. My aunt's vet that she had used for years operated on him and saved his life. He knew Tina wanted a dog, and as soon as Crash was well enough for a home, he introduced him to her, and she instantly fell in love. Because he was a puppy and still growing, the injury left him with a bit of a gimp leg and a hip that would give him a bit of trouble, but that never stopped him from what he loved best: his ball! He would play fetch for hours if you let him. Unfortunately, Crash died at the young age of six from an inoperable tumor that was growing inside of him. We all felt his loss, but none more than my aunt.

Crash was the inspiration for getting my own dog. I wanted one just like him but also like Rebecca's dog, Skye, who was a Labrador retriever. Skye had stayed close to us the first three months after we were recovered. She used to check the gate any time a car drove by the place we were staying. If the car stopped, she would come back and tell us with a loud bark. In the beginning, one of the FBI agents assigned to protect us had gotten up to check with her each time she went to the gate, but after a while the agent trusted Skye to let her know if she needed to check the gate. She was a great watchdog, but even better than that was her ability to help us all feel a little better. All qualities I wanted in my own dog. Skye and Rebecca's other little dog, named Stella, had a way of popping into the therapy sessions when they were most needed. There is nothing better than a soft dog to cuddle when you are feeling really low.

It was no secret I wanted my own dog. I even wrote about it in my first book. Rebecca called me one morning and said to look at the newspaper. I did and saw a litter of ten-week-old puppies called Boxadors for sale. Half Lab, half boxer—perfecto!

I remember the day that we went and got my dog. It was a beautiful blue-sky day, and I was so excited. So excited that I didn't realize we were being followed. It was weird because I had made a couple jokes as we left about a funny-looking car parked down the street from where we were staying. The tabloids thought they were so smart and thought they could hide in the small community we lived in. The whole community knew they were there. Tabloid reporters look exactly like you think they would: a bit greasy, rumpled, and desperate. Their cars are either rentals or beat-up old cars. Good to know if you ever think they're following you.

The farm where the puppies lived was in the middle of nowhere. I remember thinking that if the big SUV we had thought was following us was still following, I would be able to spot it. After checking in my rearview mirror, I didn't see anything suspicious.

My focus switched to the beautiful, wiggly puppies in front of me. Thinking, How will I ever choose just one out of the three cute, exuberant puppies? There were three boys left of the litter, all black with a little bit of white on their chests. One looked like it had a pattern of a butterfly on it, so I was going to pick him, but then one of them came and sat right in my lap, and I knew he was the one. He seemed right at home and very confident he was mine. Back then I could still pick him up, and so I held him close and told him we were going home. Rebecca took a picture of me and my new puppy that I later used for the back cover of my book, *A Stolen Life*. I was so happy. Finally, a dog of my own!

A car pulled across the street on this little country lane. The driver had something in his lap. It didn't look like much, and the car was a nondescript white. Rebecca and I noticed him but did not think much of it. The next day I discovered my private moment was captured for the world to see. No choice now. He had seized a part of my day. At first I felt sick. Maybe I would have to hide again. I learned about the picture from Nanny Goat. She called and told me. At first I thought I had done something wrong. I should have realized who that man was in that car. But then I realized it had nothing to do with anything I should or should not have done. He was in the wrong, not me. I had no reason to run and hide. No one would take my freedom away again.

These intrusions have happened more than once. I can't tell you I have gotten used to them because I don't think you ever can or will. Luckily, they have stopped now. The worst were when they took pictures of the girls. To me, taking pictures of my daughters was unfair game. We never asked for any of this. It's not like we are the Kardashians or anyone looking for fame. On one occasion I think someone told the tabloids where we were camping. Can you imagine that? I try not to think about that anymore; it just makes me feel terrible and reminds me of being hunted. All those years of being invisible and then suddenly I can't hide if I want to.

That day will be forever in my mind. It was the best day ever, taking my puppy home. But it also holds a negative vibe for me because we were followed and my private moment was taken from me. Taking care of a puppy was a big responsibility. Like being a mom in some ways to a new child.

We had our four cats living with us that we had rescued from the backyard we were held in. They were all from the same litter, and we had named them Zelda, Emma, Tyson, and Mousey. My cats hated me the first couple months for bringing home a big black creature that wiggled and squirmed all over them and was such an undignified creature, or so I imagine they thought. They eventually forgave me and warmed up to him. He became a big, cozy, warm blanket that they could cuddle up with. Those cats mean so much to my daughters and me. They were cared for by strangers after our recovery and then given back to us. You can't imagine what that meant to my girls and me. We lost a few cats from not being able to take them to the vet, and others we had to leave behind because rescuers could not find them. To this day, my daughters and I are very sad when we think of them. We hope they are okay and maybe even living on someone's couch, free and happy.

Those first few weeks with my new puppy were some of the worst of my life. He became deathly sick. He would be playing one minute and then get uncontrollable shivers that racked his body. He also threw up everything he would eat. I took him to the vet, and they said he had parvovirus and that only a small percentage of puppies made it through this deadly disease. I had no idea where he could have gotten it. I had taken him to the vet to get his vaccinations, and he had been strong and healthy then. A few days later he was fighting for his life. I had to leave him with the vet for him to be hooked up to IV fluids. It was so hard leaving him. The next day after a fitful night's sleep, I received a call from the vet. They told me I could come and pick him up. I was surprised he was recovering so quickly. They said they were surprised, too. They knew he was getting better when they discovered he had chewed through the IV! When I brought him home, I had to bleach the areas where he went to the bathroom because I learned that the parvo virus could live in the soil and infect the next dog. In fact, that could be how he had gotten it in the first place.

I made him chicken and rice for his dinner with a little ginger root mixed in to help calm his tummy. We slept on the couch every night together, so I could take him out to the potty because he still had the runs sometimes. I was so glad he was going to be okay, though. After that ordeal, I finally picked a name for him: Bull. Stubborn and strong just like a bull.

Beware what you name your pets. I thought I had picked such a creative name. A name that forever connected my new puppy to me and epitomized who he was. I thought, I am a Taurus, and your name shall be Bull, little puppy. He had been through much during his so-far short life. After the ordeal with parvo, Bull grew fast and so did his stubborn nature. (My mom told me that was the nickname she called me as a child.) Is that how I survived? Pure stubbornness?

Puppy-training classes came once a week. I had imagined myself being the dog whisperer and training this puppy to become the most well behaved dog in human history. Well, at the least how to sit and stay. I really wanted to prove I could train and have a well-behaved dog. As a little girl, I had promised my mom that if I ever got a dog, that's what I would do. I quickly learned that sometimes you get what you need and not what you want. My beautiful thirty-pound puppy was not easily trained. He had a mind of his own. He became very bonded to me, and I took him everywhere. At first he didn't like the car, but I gave him treats and he quickly decided he loved car rides. My trainer said I shouldn't let him off leash so much and loose on the property. She recommended keeping him tied when I wasn't home. I tried a few times, but I just couldn't.

Bull quickly decided he would follow wherever I went, and when I wasn't home instead of tying him up, which I just couldn't do, I let him be in the closed-off garden on the property. For some reason, making him do things just didn't work, but if I made it so it felt like something he decided, he learned so much quicker and it stuck. Weekly jaunts into town to work on "heel" and "come" lasted for a few months but just felt boring for us both. My dreams of being the dog whisperer died a slow death. What emerged was something far more precious to me: a friendship. We learned our own style of training after that. I anticipated his reactions and learned how to train the behaviors I needed him to have but that worked for him, too. He likes routine, and I don't. So we have compromised and worked out that sometimes we play stick at night and sometimes we play ball in the morning. He loves playing with the horses. He's still such a puppy at heart at the age of five. When the horses are in the arena, he loves to run with them on the track around the outside he has made. He's the fastest dog I have ever seen and reminds me of Crash in so many ways. I'm glad he had the opportunity to know and play with Crash before he left us.

Today Bull is a ninety-pound, sleek-muscled, happy dog. I have learned so much from him.

Like:

- My perfect walks on the beach are instead loud and sometimes sandy runs on the beach.
- Even though I have Labrador in me, water is not for everyone and don't waste it on me!
- Don't read before bed; I don't like it! (We've had to compromise on this one. Instead of going straight up on the bed, he waits till I put the book down and turn off the light.)
- Make sure you really want me when you call me or don't bother to call me.
- Love is not always perfect. Love is unconditional and free.

One day he taught me the most important lesson yet. He taught me to deal with the anxiety of not knowing where he was.

I had left for a few hours when I got a call. Mom said Bull was missing. I was in a store, maybe even Walmart, when I got the news. My heart exploded in fear. I told myself to be calm. It was going to be okay. I called Rebecca; she was in session and didn't answer. Everything went black. What if he did not return? My mind raced with every scary thought running through my head. I told myself he ran away or he was taken. Perhaps he was running down the street looking for me. What if he was lost and never came back? The terror I felt inside me made me sick. I couldn't even think straight. I told myself to keep calm. I promised myself he would be okay and that it would work out. I pushed the tears back and mentally began to prepare for searching for him. I remembered a recent picture of him I would post around town. We would find him, I told myself, struggling to keep the doubts away. I drove home in terror but pretending I was fine. Having an action plan made me feel so much better. As I drove into my driveway, the emotions welled up again. What if I couldn't find him? What if . . . Just then, there he was at the top of the driveway standing next to my mom. He saw my car and ran quickly toward me. I threw the car in park, jumped out, and ran toward him. As cheesy as it sounds, I was crying. My mom was laughing, and Bull was really no more or less excited to see me than on any other day. He jumped up (something we were still working on) and placed a big, sloppy dog kiss on my face. "Where were you?" I asked, not really expecting an answer. My mom came over and gave me a big hug. She said "Jayce, I found him in the shed out back. He must have wandered in when I went to get the gardening tools. He was right there the whole time!"

Me with new puppy.

My puppy Bull and his best friend Crash.

"Dream a Little Dream"

In the spring of 2012, my family and I were invited to New York by Diane von Fürstenberg. Her foundation, the Diller–von Fürstenberg Family Foundation, supports the DvF Awards, and she wanted to honor me and my foundation with the Inspiration Award.

The night before my flight to New York to attend the DvF Awards, I had a dream. The thought of this award was really weighing heavy on my mind for two reasons: it would be the first award I had ever received, and it would be the first time I had to give a speech in front of a lot of people. The old me, the one that lived as a captive so long in a backyard, was terrified of giving a speech and accepting an award that I felt I didn't deserve just yet. I was still in the "finding me" stage and growing into the person I wanted to be. This dream, though, made me see that the old me was a scared little girl, but the new me in the dream was capable of anything she set her mind to. It was time to let the one holding me back die.

The dream was like this:

My daughters and I are prisoners of Phillip's again. We are living in a place by the beach in a two-story house. I could see out a window where there was a maze of docks leading out to the ocean. The girls were watching The Powerpuff Girls *on TV in a room in the back. Mojo Jojo, the villain in the show, was bent on controlling the world, and I remember thinking, Wow, Mojo Jojo is just like Phillip!*

Clothes and trash were thrown everywhere, all over. All of a sudden, Phillip marches in and starts yelling, but I'm not sure what about or what he is actually saying. It just sounds like yelling, and no coherent words come out of his mouth. He leaves after a while and lies down on the couch in the next room with the Bible covering his face. Nancy is on her hands and knees on the floor cleaning. I tell her I'm leaving with the kids. I go to pack our stuff and tell the girls we are leaving. Nancy tries to stop me, and then all of a sudden Phillip is there in the room and he goes to hurt my youngest daughter, so I jump at him and knock him down and put my hands around his throat. I'm choking him. I press and press harder, and then he dies, and I wake up.

Lesson Learned!

During that trip to New York for the DvF Awards I learned a very valuable lesson. Someone can tell you not to do something all day long, but some lessons you have to learn for yourself. Drinking too much alcohol was one of those lessons for me, and the resulting hangover was punishment that I won't soon forget.

Arriving in New York felt like I was surrounded by a hive of bees swarming and buzzing everywhere. The city seemed like it was alive. There were so many people walking on the streets. A cab came to pick us up from the airport. We passed a beautiful bridge, and I got a glimpse of Central Park. I wanted to be Dora the Explorer for the day and just explore every nook and cranny of this big new city. Unfortunately, I'm actually way too cautious to try anything like that. Being a prisoner does funny things to the mind; feeling like you just can't take risks is one of them. I think it over before I do anything and usually talk myself out of it if it seems too risky. Maybe I've always been like that, but at times it's frustrating and taking chances seems like a steep mountain too high to climb. I would like to take a big risk one day and see what happens. I did go up in a balloon one day. It didn't feel like a risk, but now that I think of it, it was a little risky. I figure falling in love one day will be a risk. Will I take it?

The sounds of the city made it hard for me to concentrate on just one voice at a time. I could hear hundreds all around me. The sun reflected off the buildings and blinded my very sensitive eyes. I tried to act like this was just another day in the life of Jaycee Dugard, but it was anything but a normal day. Tall buildings and skyscrapers were everywhere I turned. I was in the land of giants. Bright yellow taxis waiting on every corner, and my favorite part of all was all the food vendors on the streets as we passed by. I wanted to jump out of the cab and try everything. I could literally smell the delicious aromas of gyros, pretzels, and churros from the vendors we passed.

Later that day, after we were checked into our hotel, Diane von Fürstenberg invited us for lunch at her shop-studio on Washington Street. Never in a million years did I think I would be meeting a famous designer like Diane. I had done some research about her before the trip. I like to be prepared and seem knowledgeable about things. So I knew a little about her before we met. As she swept into the room and embraced me in a hug that felt so warm and inviting, I immediately felt a kinship with her. She asked me about my foundation and asked how I was doing. She treated my whole family like she had known us forever. She invited us to explore the shop and pick out something and also for me to pick out something for my daughters to take back home. I picked out this fabulous purple—my favorite color—purse and two scarves for the girls. I left thinking that I had made a new friend and was very excited for the night to come.

That night I still wasn't comfortable putting on makeup or wearing pretty clothes. I picked something that I had bought at Ross that I felt comfortable in. I applied a little bit of makeup. When we arrived, we were ushered into the green room, where they served us dinner. I was so caught up in meeting everyone that I took only a few bites. Jessica Alba was there. As I'm writing this I'm thinking of the song "Girl Crush," by Little Big Town. Jessica Alba makes it easy to have a girl crush on, and, no, I don't want a girlfriend. (I have learned to be careful what I say or write. People sometimes see or hear what they want to. Or what they think I mean.) Jessica was so very lovely and down to earth. She said she had wanted to meet me. I couldn't believe it. I felt so out of place in my simple dress from Ross.

I was told that Oprah Winfrey was going to be giving me my award, and she came in to meet me. She was wearing a beautiful green dress, and I'm so short I barely came up to her chest. She said she'd always wanted to meet me and that she admired the work I was doing with my foundation. She said she was honored to be introducing me for the Inspiration Award that year.

Before the ceremony started, we were escorted to our chairs. Oprah's assistant approached me and asked if I would like to sit with her in the front row. I said thank you so much for the offer but I'd really like to sit with my family. I hope I did not insult her. Thinking about it later, she might have thought that was rude. That was not my intention. I still just simply wanted to be with my family every chance I got. I wonder, can you ever really get back eighteen years? I missed so much of my little sister growing up, learning to walk, and all those sister times. Here we were, and she is with me looking beautiful, grown-up, and so confident. How did that all happen?

As the night wore on and my time approached, I was extremely nervous. I had written an acceptance speech, and Nanny Goat sat beside me as Oprah stepped onto the stage. As her booming voice echoed through the room, I heard her introduce the founder of the JAYC Foundation, Jaycee Dugard. Wow! I can't believe I am here! Oprah continued on to say I had endured eighteen years with only a bucket . . . LOL. Yep, that's me. My nerves shot through the roof. Finally, the time came. With applause exploding in my ears, I walked up to the podium. The lights were blinding. I looked out into darkness and said the first line from my first book, *A Stolen Life:* "Let's get one thing straight! My name is Jaycee Lee Dugard!" After that I don't remember a whole lot. I finished my speech and thanked the Diane von Fürstenberg family and foundation for the award and contribution to my newly founded foundation and walked back down off the dais.

I was so nervous, and I don't think I really took the time to savor every moment. I wish I had taken more time to get to know Oprah and others at the party. I was so proud of myself for speaking in front of such a big crowd of people. It was the first speech I had ever given.

I was so relieved when it was over that I had forgotten that I hadn't eaten dinner, and when offered a glass of Champagne, I took it with gusto. I downed it within seconds. The bubbles tickled my nose and throat as I swallowed, but it was so good.

Little desserts were being passed out on trays, and I took one every time the tray passed. I also had another glass of white wine. I'm pretty sure I had another glass of Champagne, too, as the night wore on. I was very relaxed by this point and feeling pretty good. Later that night, we decided to walk and get some pizza. We plotted a course and trudged along the streets of New York to the pizza joint. I forgot to be afraid of the city. After about an hour walking, we pretty much gave up hope that we would ever find the pizza place we were looking for and settled for the one we found around the next corner. Yum, so good. We also got a bottle of wine to take back to the room. Everyone went to bed except for my sister and me, and we ended up sharing the entire bottle of wine, plus we ordered a chocolate sundae from room service. Yes, it was past midnight, but we were celebrating.

I think I passed out on the couch sometime during the night. I don't know how I made it to my room upstairs, but that's where I woke up the next morning with a splitting headache! I could barely move. The pounding in my head was so intense I thought somebody had taken a hammer to it. My eyes felt gritty and hard to open. I'm stubborn sometimes. So when Rebecca called and asked if I wanted to go out and find a Starbucks, I said yes. We planned to meet at her room and go from there.

Getting dressed was a disaster. I had two different socks, and I'm pretty sure my shoes didn't match either. I left the sanctuary of my hotel room and plotted my route to her hotel room. She was located in the fifteenth floor in another tower of the massive hotel we were in, so I had to get in the elevator and navigate across the lobby to the other set of elevators that would take me to her floor. I don't know how I made it to the first elevator. It's kind of a blur. Crossing the lobby, all I could think of was, stand up straight. I was just waiting for someone to point and shout, "Hey, look, is that Jaycee Lee Dugard with a massive hangover?"

Getting into the second elevator felt like a victory. Albeit a short-lived one. I felt like even though the light was blinding and my headache was throbbing, I could do this. I could make it. That darn elevator had other ideas for me and hurtled as fast as it possibly could and stopped at every other floor. As I watched the numbers go from 5 to 8 and stop. Oh no, people! As they entered the elevator with me, I told myself to "act cool" and not show how bad I really felt.

Up, up to 10. Ding, stop, the people got off. Whew! Up, up I went to the fifteenth floor finally. I swayed as I walked down the corridor. I felt like I was going to be sick. Keep walking, I told myself. I finally made it to room 1509. I knocked. I hear Rebecca reply, "Just a minute I'm in the bathroom." I knock again, louder this time. She shouts, "I'm coming." She opens the door, and I barrel and push right past her to the open door of the bathroom. I slammed the door and landed face first in the holy bowl of the toilet. I was very, very sick. After that, all I wanted at this point was my bed. Rebecca asked if I was okay. Nope, I was not. There would be no Starbucks for me. I asked if she could take me back to my room.

Off we went back into the hall. Not two steps from the door, and I had to throw up again, but she had already closed the door. We spotted a maid cart. Thank goodness! I headed over and grabbed a bag. I told Rebecca I couldn't possibly get back into that horrible elevator. I was convinced it wanted to kill me. She suggested the stairs, which seemed like a better option to me at the time. Every step was excruciating. My head was spinning round and round. We finally made it to the bottom, but it wasn't the lobby like I thought it would be. It was some kind of weird part of the hotel. Like behind the scenes. Were we lost? Yes, we were. Rebecca asked a passing bellman how to get to the lobby. He directed us to yet another elevator! I didn't think I could do the stairs anymore, and so taking the elevator seemed like our only option.

Sweat was dripping down my face from trying to act cool just in case someone came into the elevator with us. We finally arrived on my floor. I rushed to the door. My sister was there, bless her thoughtful heart, already holding it open for me, Rebecca had called and told them my, ah . . . situation. I was so relieved to be back in my hotel room I didn't care who knew.

We were supposed to go sightseeing that day, but I couldn't even think about that anymore. No bus rides for me. I really wanted to rest so I could at least go to the play *Wicked* on Broadway that we had gotten tickets to see that night. I didn't want to miss my first Broadway show! I told everyone to go sightseeing without me.

Shayna and Garrett, her boyfriend at the time (who later became her husband, but that's another chapter), were so nice. They went to the drugstore and got me something for my head and a bagel with cream cheese. I couldn't even think about food, but it was very sweet and I appreciated it. The bread actually helped my tummy to feel better. I spent part of the day on the bathroom floor because it felt cool. I was completely unable to get up. Such an embarrassing day for me. I don't know why I felt embarrassed. I just did. I like to be in control of myself, and I had no idea that mixing Champagne, wine, and sugar would cost me so much. Lesson learned the hard way.

You would think I would stay away from alcohol after that, but although I stayed away from it for a very long time, it did eventually creep back into my life in the form of mint mojitos! Nectar of the gods. I love the refreshing taste of citrus and mint. Best of all, it didn't give me a hangover the next morning. I pretty much stick with these. Drinking is okay, but in moderation for sure.

Me, Jessica Alba, and Diane at the DvF Awards in New York.

Meeting Diane Sawyer in New York.

Walk the Plank

You wouldn't think walking could give you nightmares. Well, I sure had some nightmarish dreams about walking after I was kidnapped. For a while I had this dream about having to "walk the plank." In the dream I would start up the hill from my house in South Lake Tahoe. It would always be perfectly sunny, not a cloud in the sky in this recurring dream, and I would have on the same outfit I was taken in. Pink stretch pants and white T-shirt with a kitty on it. My favorite outfit, actually; how ironic. Phillip burned all my clothes, so I never saw that outfit again except in this dream/nightmare.

All of a sudden I would be blindfolded but still walking up the hill. I kept walking and walking and walking all the while with no sight whatsoever. Total blackness even though I knew it was sunny out. I could feel myself start to panic, but there was nothing I could do. All of a sudden, there was no more road and I could feel myself falling in midair just as if I had stepped off a plank. I would always wake up as I felt myself hit water and start to sink.

I haven't had this dream in years. I was afraid to walk places by myself when I was first recovered. During the building of the court case against Phillip and Nancy Garrido, and before the trial phase, I was asked to go up to Tahoe and review for the police and prosecutors exactly how I was kidnapped by Phillip and Nancy on June 10th, 1991. Rebecca came with me on this trip, and I'm so glad I had her support.

I think walking that hill was actually cathartic for me, even though I thought it would be traumatic. Facing my fears and knowing that I could walk the same path and nothing bad would happen was good for me. That's also when Rebecca figured out my obsession with pinecones and why I would ask friends to bring me one from places they would visit. It happened like this: I was sitting in the car talking about that day, Rebecca runs over with a pinecone and says, "Look! This was in the place he grabbed you! Duh, no wonder you want pinecones. It must have been the last thing you touched before Phillip pulled you into the car!" After that, my obsession made so much more sense and turned into a very powerful symbol of new beginnings for me.

Months into my recovery process, I had my first solo walk. It wasn't even really planned. The principal of my youngest daughter's school asked to meet with me, and since the school was just a few blocks away, I decided to walk. Rebecca called on my way there, and I told her I was walking and on my way to meet with the principal. She seemed a bit awed on the phone, and I didn't really know why. She said she would see me soon and hung up.

I really honestly wasn't thinking much about anything during the walk until I reached the halfway point. And that's when it hit me! Wow, look at me! I'm walking the neighborhood by myself. I finally understood why Rebecca sounded like that on the phone. As I started my way down the street that would bring me to the school, I could see two people waiting for me. I admit I was a little embarrassed at first. I was so proud of myself, though, and couldn't stop the smile on my face no matter how much I tried to look cool and casual.

Rebecca had filled in the principal of the school, who knew me and my story and was taking such good care of my daughter in his school. I think he felt honored to be there for my maiden voyage. As I got nearer, I could see them smiling, too, and that made me feel so good. I made it. And I knew I could do it again . . . and I have.

Later, Rebecca told me that they got a little worried when they saw a highway patrol car coming down the street. Just as they started to wonder where I was, there I was. I had just turned the corner as the patrol car passed.

Early into my recovery, I still had my entourage following me: FBI agents, victim advocates, etc. One day that sticks out in my mind started out in Rebecca's office for a therapy session, but I was just feeling restless. Rebecca picked up on it and suggested a walk up a nearby road that had a steep incline. I was intrigued and thought it sounded great. As we all piled into the black SUVs with the tinted windows, the plan was Rebecca and I would walk a little ahead so we could talk on the way up, and the FBI and victim advocates would stay behind us to give me privacy.

The walk was hard. And my thighs and calves started to burn quickly. But the burn felt good and talking about the past became easier as we walked side by side. The beautiful view helped when I talked about the really awful parts Phillip made me do. I was really out of breath, and talking was getting harder. By the time we reached the top with not a soul in sight, I realized I had talked almost the whole way up. I was out of breath and huffing and puffing, but I felt clean and refreshed.

Rebecca showed me the ritual of touching the silver plaque on the tree at the top. That little ritual has stayed with me every time I make the climb to the top. On our way down, we realized that the others had not made it even halfway up as we came down. I remember sleeping really well that night. To this day, exercise is important to me. I love to eat, too, so dieting is not really an option for me, and I'd rather exercise than restrict my diet, so I will probably never be model thin, but that suits me just fine as long as I am in shape. Exercise releases endorphins, which make you feel good and oftentimes enhance your outlook on life in general. Exercise has helped me cope with stress and ward off depression when it comes. I never want to be that person I was in the backyard that hardly ever moved. Granted, that was not a choice that was mine to make. I was a prisoner.

My mind feels more alert when I move and exert myself, and the outlook on the day is improved. When I don't exercise, I feel it. Especially around the holidays when I tend to overeat and not make an effort to exercise, and once you stop, it's hard to get back to a routine. When I'm a log on the couch all day, my legs get all crampy and seem to say, Hey get up and move, girl!

I went out of my comfort zone for a while and decided to get a gym membership. I usually do not like to feel like I'm being watched in any way whatsoever. I was really opposed to exercising where people I did not know could see me. I get embarrassed easily.

The decision to join came about when my oldest daughter wanted to join. She had been on the cross-country team at her school and loved the feeling exercise gave her. I thought it would be a fun thing to do together and would help me overcome my shyness, which I wanted to get over. I think age helps with this fear because when I was little, I had it really bad. It was hard to make friends, and my friends ended up coming to me, not the other way around. I was always too scared. Being older, I have noticed that this has changed a lot. Not so much when I was a captive but being around Rebecca and seeing her confidence has helped me grow. And so I joined the gym. And you know what else? I went to Zumba classes. Yep, that's right. I tried to rhumba and samba my way to fitness, ladies and gentlemen. The worst part was I could tell I was really bad at it from the gigantic mirror in front of me. But it was fun, and I realized no one was staring at me . . . like at all. Nope. And do you know why? Because they were looking at themselves in that big ol' gigantic mirror that shows everything!

I really liked taking those classes in the gym, and I kept it up for about six months. Then I realized I enjoyed hiking and working out with my friends better. I was very proud of myself for trying it out, though. It helped a whole lot in my confidence to try new things and not to care what I looked like. Also because I was doing something great for me. And that felt good.

I recommend finding a buddy to keep you motivated. When my best friend, Jessie, comes to visit, we try to do something active, and to this day I still take many hikes and exercise with my mentor, Rebecca. My sister got me a Fitbit for Christmas and I love it. It tends to really motivate me to meet my step goal. If I see that I haven't quite reached it at the end of the day, I will get on the elliptical. Which I would not have thought to do before. It's something about the feeling of accomplishing something that feels so good. And I find I sleep better, too.

Don't Judge

After receiving my first horse, I really wanted another one for my daughters to ride. That was the plan anyway, but it didn't quite happen like I thought it would. Instead, another horse came into my life and taught me about love.

His name was Ed and he had only one eye. The other was lost to a tumor. He was a beautiful red Arabian, and I loved him the first day I laid my two eyes on him. I found him in the local paper for sale and asked Rebecca if she would go with me to check him out.

We arrived at the address and were surprised that the horse and his companion, an aged pony, were living quite literally in someone's backyard. I did get some flashbacks of being captive in Phillip's backyard. This was a very small yard for a horse. The owner had had them for her kids, but they had grown and so the horses were just there living out the rest of their lives with no place to wander free. She wanted something better for them and so had opted to sell them both. I didn't realize that they were a package deal until that moment. The thought of two new horses was a little overwhelming.

Ed was a pretty old guy, I learned, but as sweet as can be. I was still kind of afraid of the size of horses back then and didn't just get on any that I didn't know. But for some reason, Ed exuded trust from his whole being and I must have felt that. When the owner asked if I would like to ride him, I said I would. I walked around on Ed in that backyard and thought of all the reasons why this was a bad idea: You are older than I thought you were, I thought to myself. You come with an old pony. The pony is thirty-eight years old. You are no spring chicken yourself at the age of twenty-five. I was looking for a horse my daughters could ride, but you have only one eye. Margie, my horse trainer, will kill me for bringing you home. She will think I've gone insane. The list was piling up in my head. There were many reasons why I shouldn't have wanted him.

I decided to sleep on my decision to bring him home. That night, I had a dream that Ed was already mine and living with me. It felt so right that I couldn't ignore the feeling of rightness with him. So the next morning my decision was made, and Ed and his longtime companion, a pony we named Dusty, came home to my barn to live with Cowboy.

I have never regretted my decision to bring a one-eyed horse home. Dusty, unfortunately, did not live very long, only a year with us. His passing was traumatic. He didn't have many teeth left and was prone to choke. One day the choke got really bad and he also colicked. Colic is a term used to describe many stomach issues with horses. The vet told me Dusty's insides were all twisted up. It was the first time I had to make the decision to let a horse pass. Seeing Dusty suffer was so hard, and I knew that it was time. I like to think he loved his time here with us.

Years later, losing Ed to colic was an even harder moment to face. I had grown to love Ed so much over the years. He was so much a part of barn life for everyone.

He was a very stoic guy, and I didn't know that he was in pain until the very last moments of his life. Some choices I would rather not have to make. One of those decisions is whether your horse is in so much pain that it is better to end his life. I had made the decision with Dusty and now I faced it again. Making the decision to end Ed's life was like sticking a knife through my heart and pulling it out while it was still beating. I don't want to remember that pain, but it still shows up and it's hard to fight the tears.

One time Rebecca's horse, Freesia, colicked. I am usually cool under pressure, and I have never passed out in my life unless under extreme stress. It had only been a few months since the traumatic death of my beloved Ed, so when I saw Freesia lying on the ground rolling, it reminded me so much of Ed. I felt like I would pass out from seeing her lying there. Luckily, she was a lot younger and we were able to pull her through the colic.

Over the years that Ed was in my life, I watched people have various reactions to him. For me, I feel like he has redefined my idea of what a horse should be. I used to think horses were just for riding, but I have discovered that they are much more. A horse "joining up" with you on the ground gives you such a sense of connection and victory. Two feelings that have not been abundant in my life.

Bringing Ed home was one of the first big decisions I made when I moved into my new house. I have always doubted myself. After all, living as someone's captive is not the best self-esteem booster. Even after six years, I still question myself. Sometimes I feel like some people think I can't make my own choices without the input of others. I see no harm in getting other people's opinions about things and then coming to my own choice in the matter. I was not three when I was taken! I was eleven, and even though I was still young, I still knew there was more to life than Barbie dolls and birthdays. I knew my mom made a lot of tough choices. I knew it was hard being a single parent. We were lucky to live with my grandparents until I was six. I knew my mom worked hard to get us our own apartment. I knew we didn't have a lot of money, and most of it went to bills and something called taxes. I knew a lot by the time Phillip and Nancy kidnapped me, but I admit I didn't know it all.

After our rescue, it kind of felt like some people thought I would probably be stupid. I think a lot of people have underestimated me over the years and have judged my abilities harshly and inserted their own personal opinions about what I should be and who I can be. I like to think I have proven them wrong. After all, I do run my own foundation!

I try never to judge people or make unfair assumptions, because that is not the way I want to be treated. Although I must admit I do judge Phillip and Nancy. I can't help but judge everything they ever did. There was this one time when Phillip took us to the San Francisco wharf to set up for a "CAN You Hear Me?" demo. Which in itself was so stupid, him trying to get others to listen to his "black box" to see if they could hear him talking through it! Phillip would have someone put on headphones that were hooked up to a recording of static noise. He would then mouth the words "Can you hear me." Then you were supposed to hear the words being spoken through the recording. Ridiculous! Right . . . Nancy was one of the ones that could hear this so-called ability. He got others to say they could hear it, too, or so he told me, but who knows what they were really hearing or just sharing in his imagined delusion. Give me a break. But that's what his delusional mind had made up, and we were setting up a booth on the wharf for it.

One time, there was a dad and his daughter, and she was crying about not wanting to go on the 3-D amusement ride they had on Pier 39. I could hear the dad encouraging his daughter to try it and that he would be right there with her, but she continued to cry. As they walked away, Phillip said to me that he should not make his daughter do anything that was scary. That made me so annoyed! I said, "But she needs to learn there are scary things, and it is better to do it with someone that loves you than have to deal one day with those scary things on her own"—like I did, I wanted to add but didn't. He said I was wrong and scaring a little girl was wrong. What a hypocrite, I wanted to shout. What have you been doing all these years, you pervert? I still think I was right. I would much rather experience scary things with a loved one than by myself. You never know what another person is going through. I might be wrong, but who's to judge. My decision to bring Ed home could have been one of those decisions, but I don't think so.

Dusty and Ed had been together for some twenty-odd years, I was told. Dusty was an ornery ol' pony with the spirit of a young stud. My youngest daughter enjoyed walking around on him and trusted him completely. Ed had a very trusting soul, and even though he couldn't see me from one side, he still trusted me to be there. I gained a lot of confidence just being around him. Some friends have told me that they didn't realize he had one eye until I told them. Others have felt uncomfortable looking at his missing eye or wanted to know why it's missing in the first place.

One day a friend was walking with him in the arena. I noticed, however, that Ed was trying to face my friend on his blind side and every time he did, she would move back to his seeing eye side. After a few minutes of this, I asked why she wouldn't walk with him on his blind side because it was clear to me what he wanted and felt comfortable doing. She said it made her uncomfortable that he couldn't see her, but she also realized that she didn't feel like she had the right to the trust Ed was showing her. Once she said it, though, she was able to let it go and together they resumed their walk.

I have learned so many valuable lessons from the horses in my life. I've learned not to take myself too seriously and to live in the moment. I used to have a problem with "checking out." I've often asked myself, what does that mean? Well, I think for me, "checking out" was too much self-reflection and not enough practical experience dealing with people. Where I would sometimes look like I'm staring off into space would really be me just thinking about something really hard and not really noticing if there were people around. After so many years by myself I wasn't really used to talking or having conversations. Horses make you be totally present, and communication and conversations with them are a must. They insist, really. Which has helped me to improve in so many ways.

Ed making faces

Ed running

Say It Good (Sid).

Confessions of an Imperfect Person
(or Where the Heck Are the Minis?!)

—————————————————————————

It looked like it was going to rain. Not good for a day we had plans to take our miniature horses, Mister and Aurora, to a school a few miles away. As part of the JAYC Foundation's "Just Ask Yourself to Care!" School Groups, a team of us goes into schools and teaches a group of ten to twelve kids all about the importance of caring for one another in school and their communities, respect for themselves and others, how to keep themselves safe, and above all, to be aware of their surroundings!

So as we loaded up the minis for a trip out to see the kids, we didn't know what the day had in store for us. Some days teach you more lessons than you ever thought you needed, and this was one of those days. It sprinkled throughout the day, but nothing major. The kids were excited to see the miniature horses, and each had a turn doing the exercise with them. The minis were helping us learn boundaries and how much space sometimes we need to feel safe.

The day went pretty well, and we loaded the minis for the trip back to the barn. The minis didn't want to get in the trailer and were hard to convince to step up into it. It took a lot of coaxing and horse cookies, but we finally got them in. By then, it was getting really late and the sun was starting to set.

I followed the truck and trailer in my car, and all of a sudden I saw smoke coming from the front of the truck. Oh no! The truck was overheating! We all pulled over in a residential neighborhood and assessed the damage. Looked like we could not drive the truck home. How were we going to get the horses home? We didn't have another truck to pull the trailer. We could hear the minis getting really restless in the back, and so we took them out. We tried calling some mechanics, but it was late and no one was answering. We were desperate, so I thought, Hey, let's try to put them in the back of my SUV.

Mister, one of the minis, had grown up riding in the back of a station wagon and was more than willing to jump in. As he jumped in, he slipped on the hard plastic, and Aurora would not even attempt it. We decided it was too dangerous and gave up on the idea.

As we sat around trying to think of ideas, we looked around the neighborhood and got another idea. I saw a man working in his front yard. He had a pretty big-looking truck in his driveway and so we thought, Hey, it's worth a try. We went over and asked if he could pull our horse trailer home. He replied in broken English that he would, but would it be quick? Quick, we ask? Yes, he said, he wanted to watch the World Series, which would be starting soon. We told him where we lived and begged him for his help. He agreed but still seemed a little reluctant. But at least he said yes. We were so relieved.

As he hitched the trailer, we realized he really didn't understand much English but seemed like a really nice guy, and his kids were there, too. He started to pull away and shouted out the window, "Where are they going again?" We gave him the address.

As he pulls away, Rebecca and I look at each other and realize we had just let a complete stranger take our minis, and we didn't get a name or phone number or anything! Panic started to set in. We had to stay and wait for the tow truck to tow our truck, and as soon as he arrived, we took off in my car. We were really getting worried wondering if we had made a mistake trusting this stranger.

On the way back we called our friend, the chief of police, of course! Because when a person that has already been the victim of kidnap and a psychologist that has worked with said victim become scared, we get kind of silly. I'm sure he thought we were complete idiots for calling him and telling him what we had just done. I wanted to know if we could issue an Amber Alert and was only half joking. He stayed calm, which helped us to stay calm. He also was the voice of reason and said, Why don't we see if he does bring them home before we report them missing? Why don't we look around the neighborhood and call him back if we didn't find them? Hmm, I guess we could do that.

We called home and asked if the minis had arrived. No minis. Maybe he was just slow in getting there. He looked trustworthy. He had his two kids with him. Surely, he is a good person and will bring our minis home, right? We felt like complete idiots. As we approached the local market, we spotted them! Yay! we shouted in unison. He and the kids were out petting the minis in the parking lot. He had not remembered the address and hoped we would find him. And we did! He seemed a little irritated about missing the game, but otherwise was so very nice.

He followed us back to the house, where he unhitched and left for home with just our "thank yous" for payment. He wouldn't accept anything else. For a program that teaches kids awareness of their surroundings, we sure failed that day. But at least we got our sweet minis back! And I learned that there are really good strangers out there and not all of them are bad like Phillip told me.

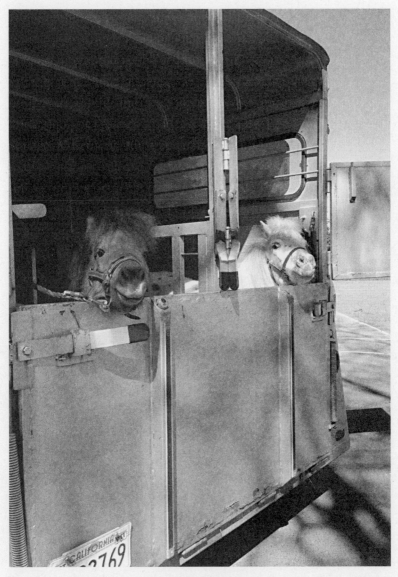

Mister and Aurora.

Addiction

Yes, I will admit it. I have fallen into the trap. I am an addict. I never thought I would succumb, but here I am confessing my sin. I am hopelessly and endlessly addicted to . . . Starbucks. There, I said it. I've admitted it. They say that's the first step. It started out innocently enough. Peppermint Mocha Frappuccinos; maybe once in a blue moon a passion fruit iced tea.

My mom goes for the vanilla lattes, but I'm not a coffee drinker. Actually, I kind of hated the smell of coffee for a while. I never understood my mom's obsession with coffee. Coffee always smelled to me like burnt socks, which I do not find appealing in any way. But after discovering the amazing creations you can achieve with coffee, I am a convert. Not a total convert. I don't like it black or with just cream. No, I like the incredibly sweet kind. I love the rich, sweet flavor of my favorite coffee beverage, caramel macchiato, with extra caramel drizzle! My oldest daughter turned me on to these when I started a low-carb diet. Now even though I don't totally stick to low-carb, although I try, it is my go-to drink. Also on my list is the seasonal pumpkin spiced latte, which I am considering how it will taste iced, and salted caramel mochas, too. Which I am quite sure are not good for me, but every once in a while I will splurge because I can if I want to!

Sometimes I can't even believe I'm thinking this way. Six years ago, caramel macchiato was not in my vocabulary at all. I was just surviving on a day-to-day basis with no trips to Starbucks in my future. I had never even been to one before. Have you ever been in a situation that seems totally hopeless and you can never imagine your life any other way? That was me. Life was like one giant roulette wheel. Although you knew the wheel would always be round, have numbers, and be red and black, you didn't know where that little ball bouncing on the wheel would end up. That's how it felt to be Phillip and Nancy's captives. Perhaps the day would be okay and you could wake up without Phillip yelling at imaginary voices in his head, or perhaps you woke to the annoying Nancy complaining what a mess the room was and insisting the girls clean it up. Most days landed on the same number and color and would drag on and on with no relief in sight of ever ending. That wheel was not kind to me or my daughters. I hated it, and life was so scary, dull, and unpredictable all at the same time. Some days I still feel like I'm living a dream and I will wake up and the nightmare that was my prison will be my reality and all this will be gone. Life now is very different. Days feel like an endless big sky full of fluffy white clouds and possibilities. The clouds change shape and sometimes bring rain, but every day is a day that can be filled with the things I like to do.

"Oh So Pretty"

I met my best friend, Jessie, at the age of four. We immediately discovered our mutual love of all things "pretty." Or to clarify, what our young minds thought was pretty. Pretty hats from the thrift store—mine a cute little side number complete with feather and veil and hers a sophisticated floppy wide brim with pretty pink ribbon.

We would spend hours dressing up in our moms' high heels and grown-up dresses. Makeup was applied when our moms were not looking, and when we deemed it time to make our debut, hand in hand we would come out and pose for the camera, displaying our cheesiest smiles. To us, we were beautiful. At six and five, this was our way of connecting and playing. Where this sense of beauty came from, I don't know. Maybe from our moms, whom we both looked up to, maybe from TV, maybe from everything we had taken in during our lives so far.

Years and many, many shall I say "events" later, "pretty" feels different to me. I have had too many life experiences for it ever to be as simple as it was for me at six. Has my sense of beauty been tainted? Well, in a nutshell, yes, it has. When a psycho grown-up man that has kidnapped you and taken you away from everything you have known and loved and forces you to "dress up" and put on makeup for his personal fantasies of having sex with a child— a very scared and afraid child, I might add—your viewpoint can change. I know mine has.

This is a tangent, but something is very contradictory to me here. Why would someone who has kidnapped a child of eleven then force her to dress up for him and put on lots of makeup and high heels? What's the point of kidnapping a child and then try- ing to make her look older? I know the answer to that is control. It is easier to control a child than it is an adult. Still the whole thing is disgusting, but from the news, I know it happens more than any of us would like to think about.

In all his sick and perverted ways, Phillip did make me realize that we had two very different versions of beauty. I remember one night when he dressed me up and I was crying, not loudly, but I could feel the hot tears streaming down my face. I was smearing the makeup job he had done on me, but I just could not hold the tears back. I could tell he was agitated, and I knew I had to stop crying. I was scared of what would happen if I didn't. Phillip looked at me and asked, "What are you crying for?" and I told him I felt ugly. I remember he looked at me and said, "You look beautiful. Here, I will show you. Look into the mirror." Well, I looked.

Plato wrote, "Beauty lies in the eyes of the beholder." That must be true because what I saw as beauty and what Phillip saw as beauty were completely different things. I don't doubt he thought I was pretty that night. His creation. The girl he took from a bus stop. A girl he controlled and could be anything he wanted. He was proud of the way I looked, and he couldn't see why I didn't see what he saw. All I saw was a very frightened girl who I didn't even recognize with mascara running down her cheeks and the saddest face I had ever glimpsed staring back at me. I had to avert my eyes quickly and nod my head in agreement; I did not want to provoke the sleeping dragon.

To this day when I think about society's views of beauty, I think back on that day and I think something changed for me. Looking at myself for those split seconds, I realized that beauty would never be a simple thing to me and that I would never agree with Phillip about anything . . . ever.

I think we all see beauty in our own way, and it really is "in the eyes of the beholder." I've learned not to define beauty simply as what someone looks like or wears but by what that person does and aspires to. Not to say I don't love wearing beautiful clothes and buying the coolest new shoes and dressing up nicely now and then. Makeup is fun to experiment with, and I do enjoy wearing it on occasion.

It's no longer a question of "I have to" for me now but a question of "Do I want to?" For me, it has taken time to distinguish the two, because even with the freedom I have now, the pressures of our society and what we define as pretty and acceptable and the "norm" in our culture is very judgmental. Women wear makeup, they wear high heels (although I'm not sure why because they are so uncomfortable!), and we all want to have and wear the latest fashions and be socially accepted. These things take a toll on our sense of beauty as a whole, and many of us get lost in it. I do, too. But life is a teacher, and although remembering those hor-rible nights Phillip put me through is hard, it is still a reminder. It's a reminder that beauty can be seen or felt in many different ways. You can be seen with too much or too little, and most judge beauty by what they see. I'm guilty of this.

I once judged a horse by its color only. It wasn't until I got to know him that I saw what a great horse he could be. I got him in 2013. His name is Say It Good, or Sid for short, and he's a chest-nut quarter horse.

At first, I saw only a plain, drab brown horse, but when I was helped to look deeper and discovered his beauty, I saw a horse with a big heart and tons of potential. When I look at him today, it's funny; I no longer see just a brown horse. I see the multitude of colors he has in his coat, I see gentle eyes and a horse that feels the beauty around him.

Beauty is all around us. To redefine beauty in ourselves and our families is not an easy thing. I fear we are all lost in a way, and although we try to remember what's truly beautiful in the world, we all at one time lose sight of it. We all get caught up in the see-ing aspect of what's beautiful. The trick is to feel the beautiful as well as see it and find the balance in between.

Where does our definition of beauty come from? One of the biggest fears I have is that society dictates our sense of beauty, and for those who have no moral compass, their sense of beauty is askew and warped, and they will never truly see or feel what true beauty is. I'm still learning what that means for me, so I can't tell

Me and Jessie playing dress-up.

you any words of wisdom. All I know is that every day I am alive and free is beautiful, and when I look in the mirror now, I don't see that ugly broken child I was and who Phillip tried his best to create because he thought that was beautiful. No, I don't see her. I just simply see the beauty in me.

This got me thinking of how animals define beauty versus us humans and how drastically different these opinions are. Animals don't see beauty or judge us based on it. If a cat is comfortable with you and trusts you, it does not care what you look like. You could have a missing eye or two missing eyes or a freakish pimple on your face, and the horse you are riding or brushing will not care one bit. Animals teach us the meaning of beautiful every day. Do you take the time to listen?

In Plain Sight

The roaring of the crowd at a basketball game is deafening! My first basketball game was the Warriors versus the Kings. Little did I know that this game would herald the end of a losing streak for my team. Perhaps I am lucky after all! Just kidding. I think the faith and hope of their fans is what brought them out of the slump. Kind of like the hope my mom had for me and her never giving up hope that I would one day come back to her. That kind of hope can move mountains.

I had never been to a basketball game before, even when I was little. This was a first. We had gotten courtside tickets, and I was very excited to see my first game. I didn't realize the cameras would be so close, though. I was still paranoid about being recognized and felt on the hot seat as I sat there and watched the game.

What is it with me and being recognized? I just wanted to enjoy the game. Over the years I have been to a football game with my aunt ("Go Chargers!"), and a Lady Gaga, a Beyoncé, and a Garth Brooks concert. These concerts were all very unique and different in their own ways, but I enjoyed them all. Lady Gaga, while on the strange side, is a person I admire for being herself in all things. Garth Brooks is an amazing performer, and he gives everything he has to every performance. I love the way he is so into his wife. I would love to have a man love me the way Garth loves Trisha.

You are probably wondering if I think I can even have a relationship with a man. Good question. Although hard to answer because I can't see the future. HAHA. I'm not actively seeking love, and I refuse to do dating sites. I do feel like I'm totally capable of having a relationship one day. I don't feel so damaged that I am totally put off by the idea. I just don't know. I see my daughters having relationships, and I feel like one day when the time is right I will meet the right person for me. I like romance and fairy-tale junk, so my expectations are pretty high nowadays. So unless you ride a beautiful white stallion, can stand with me to slay all our dragons, and make me a princess, you are pretty much out of luck.

I have never even been on a date before! The only boy ever to ask me out was ten, and I was nine. My mom and I were living in an apartment complex, and he lived with his dad. They had the cutest Chow Chow dog with a curly tail. I loved his dog and the boy—I think his name was Tony—was really fun to play tag with. We would run around the apartment complex for hours as he chased me and Jessie, who also lived in the same complex.

One day as I was playing in my room, he came in and asked if I wanted to go out on a date with him. I remember laughing and thinking, That's so funny. Why did he want to take me on a date? He couldn't even drive! Back then I was painfully shy and wasn't thinking about boys in a romantic way. To me, he was just a friend. I was nine and probably a very young nine. I didn't really know what to say and so I turned him down. I kind of regret that now, but who knew that would be my only opportunity.

That day at my first basketball game, I was in plain sight of the multitude of cameras practically the whole time. But nobody noticed, which I was glad for because I was just there to enjoy the game.

But that day got me to thinking how "in plain sight" I was during my years in captivity and nobody noticed me. Phillip had a number of parole agents throughout the years, but none of them just went a little deeper into their job and noticed us. It felt like nobody cared enough to look deeper into a convicted sex offender's life. Or maybe they just didn't want to offend him or, heaven forbid, offend his wife and his mother.

The truth of the matter is my whole life was impacted with this one heinous crime that affected not only my entire family but others in the world as well. In my case, the effects are on the inside and outside. Although therapy started practically on day one for me, it is not until now, years later, that I am coming to terms with just how terrified I really was and how I couldn't let myself feel that terror when I was kidnapped and throughout my captivity. My instincts, intuition, internal thought process, whatever it was, kept my real terror at bay so I could function and survive.

In 2013, I made the decision to sue the federal government for its role in my kidnapping. It was not an easy decision to make. The whole process—the depositions, the psychological testing—had the side effect of bringing all the hidden terrors to the surface of my mind.

After I was deposed, I had some terrible nightmares about Phillip. In one I call the "shadow dream," Phillip was a shadow, and I was running through a maze with mirrors around every corner. There would be this dark, very tall and skinny shadow in my peripheral vision. Always looming and coming closer as I tried to run away.

I also have waking terrors. I am awake and doing something like working in my garden and for a split second I feel like I am in a dream and any minute I will wake and my now life will be taken from me and I will wake to my backyard prison that consumed more than half my life.

Being deposed was hard, with some very weird lines of questioning that I could not have predicted. Like "Did you ever plant flowers on the Garrido residence besides around your tent?" What kind of question is that, I thought to myself. Or my favorite one: "Do you prefer the agressive animals or the more calm, docile animals?" Or the one about my book: "You say 'I never really have nightmares. Only once in a while.' Did you have a lot of nightmares when you were at the Garrido residence?" Nice having your words thrown in your face like that, but I looked her in the eyes and said, "At the time of writing this, I lied to myself quite a bit and I wouldn't admit to myself that just because I wasn't waking up from nightmares doesn't mean that I constantly didn't think about what he had done." I don't know exactly what she was trying to get at with these questions. Did she think a day goes by in my life that my captivity does not affect me? Doesn't she realize that when I wrote my book that it was a power statement I made, and power statements help move us toward our goals but to achieve these goals takes time and a lot of hard work has to be done, and that doesn't happen overnight? So, yes, the nightmares are fading, and I live a good life, but scars are scars and can be healed but never go away completely. My scars are not visible, but I can feel them. They are reminders every day to live life to the fullest because you never know what can happen. You can use them and they can become a symbol.

At one point the attorney even called me "Miss Garrido." Maybe this was a genuine mistake on her part or maybe she was trying to rile me or throw me off. For what purpose, though? It's not like I was on trial. I wasn't the one that committed a crime, as I feel my government did, and my feelings and thoughts were clear as to why I was there and putting myself in this chair of endless questions and arduous process. So was that just a slip or something more sinister that I was not prepared for? The result of her calling me that vile name was nothing but a correction from me and an apology from her. In the end, the depo lasted seven long hours.

It was hard to involve my daughters in this daunting process. But we all felt strongly about justice being served. The deposition of my oldest daughter was even worse, with questions as bizarre as whether she was a member of the gay and straight alliance and if that meant she was gay. What? What business is that of yours, and what does that have to do with anything about this case?

I understand the prosecutor had a job to do. And, hopefully, that's all she was thinking—that this was her job. And nothing she said was personal. I just feel she missed seeing us as human beings and did only see us as a job. To her, we were just another case to win, and maybe I'm naïve and this is all we are to the government. What if our government doesn't see us as people, as individuals? What if we are all just cases to be won or lost? Well, if there is one thing I'd like to change it's that we are seen for the people we are, not just as words on a page.

Disgusted

In the spring of 2013, I was in Washington at a dinner with family and friends when I learned the story of the Cleveland girls, as they were dubbed in the media, who were kidnapped by Ariel Castro. Yet again the media putting out what sounds flashy instead of what would be appropriate. These were three grown women who I'm sure didn't want to be called "girls."

The next night I would receive the Hope Award from the National Center for Missing and Exploited Children (NCMEC). Nanny Goat received the news first and filled us in on the details as she knew them. I was stunned and amazed. Others like me and Elizabeth Smart! I was happy but at the same time deeply saddened that history repeated itself in a way again. In my acceptance speech, I said, "What an amazing time to be talking about hope!" It was a hopeful event, but the occasion also marked the beginning of new lives in the world, those of Michelle, Gina, and Amanda and her daughter. I felt a kinship toward Amanda because she too had a daughter, and I had had two. I knew, though, that their lives were very different from mine, and I didn't dare speculate on what she went through.

This was just the beginning of them making their own decisions, I knew all too well. Right away with their first appearances on TV, they all struck me as being hopeful for their futures and all that life had to offer. That evil man took their decisions away from them, and now they had that ability again. What would they do with it? I asked myself that night. Phillip took my decision making away from me, too. Would they feel like I did at times? Unsure of themselves, but with time things would get a bit easier. It makes me so mad to think of predators out in the world, preying on other people and ruining their lives for their own benefit. I feel like what gives these fuckers any right to our lives? What makes these bastards of the world feel they can control anyone but themselves? Maybe that's the problem: these assholes can't even control themselves and therefore feel the need to control others. What creates this type of person? What circumstances, events, or mental process creates the Garridos and Castros of the world? This is a question that affects us all, and I believe it needs an answer. But how do you find an answer to this question so that history will stop repeating itself?

I think the interview Michelle did on the *Dr. Phil* show was what she needed to do for herself to move on from her trauma. She's taking back her life. The next thing is deciding if that decision is truly the one in your heart or if it's what others want you to do. My hope for her is that she is doing what's right for her and her son. Moving forward after so long in captivity is not easy. Everybody wants to be your friend, and that can make matters complicated to figure out who is truly with you for the right and honest reasons. Some days will seem easier than others, and the days will not always be sunny. But even on your cloudiest rainy day, there is hope that you are alive and you can do something good to help others because of the fact of your survival. The simple fact that you survived a horrible situation gives people hope that they can survive their own situations. It is also a lesson to be thankful for what you have and those you love because it could be so much worse. I had the opportunity to meet Gina and Amanda at a recent NCMEC Hope Award ceremony. They had just released their own book entitled *Hope*. I was glad to have the time to get to know them a little, and although we had different experiences, the trauma is much the same and takes time to heal. I hope they find what they need in their lives. We also met Senator John McCain, and he said to us, "I know a little something about being alone, too." Wow! What a totally amazing moment in my life to connect on such a level with not only one fellow survivor but three! It taught me to remember to enjoy my life and take comfort that we have all been through shit, but the important thing is we survived, and not only that, we have rewarding and enriching lives to lead and inspire others with. Maybe if we all started throwing happiness in the air instead of violence, the world would be a much better place to live in, and deranged, psycho men like Ariel Castro, the man who kidnapped Gina, Amanda, and Michelle, and the Phillip Garridos of the world would not even be a thought.

Barbies Are Good for the Soul

Even after six years of freedom, I admit I still get nervous about being recognized in public. Even though I know people are just people and want to say the right thing, it still goes through my mind not to be seen. That mantra was so much a part of my life that it is sometimes still hard to overrule it with common sense. My biggest fear was that somehow Phillip would find a way to take my kids from me if I broke the rules in any way. I don't have that fear to hold me back anymore. I have new ones, but those seem simple in comparison.

However, over the years of freedom, many people have helped to put my fear of being seen into perspective. Like the time I went through airport security and the male security guard that checks your license and plane ticket looked at me funny. I thought to myself, Oh man, he recognizes my name, because really, who doesn't? Or so I thought at the time. He shocked me and threw me for a loop when he said, "Oh, wow you're from that Big family." At first it took me a second to get what he meant, and then it dawned on me: he thinks I'm from the Duggar family and one of eighteen siblings! Again, he speaks up and says, "I thought you would be taller." I was M-O-R-T-I-F-I-E-D! I wanted to shout at him, "How rude!" but refrained from making a scene. Instead, I laughed it off and proceeded with my life—all five feet of me! I realized it's not so bad being recognized . . . not.

Another moment I got a little too into myself was one time when my mom and I took a trip to explore the city. As we perused the streets, a couple came up to us a little sheepishly, and I thought, Oh here we go. I have been recognized for sure! I told myself to act cool and casually, like this happens all the time. The young woman says, Hello. Mom and I both say hi. The lady then asks in a strong accent if I would take a picture. Of course, I reply. So I go over to the couple and put my arm around the young lady's neck as the gentleman looks at me funny. They both turn to me and say, We mean can you take a picture of us? Oh no! I thought they wanted a picture with me. How embarrassing. As my face turns red, I try to recover my composure, and my mom takes the shot of the happy couple and off they go, probably baffled as to my strange behavior. Lesson learned: Don't ever assume!

There are times in life you realize that you are not the center of the universe and that the person with you might be. Especially when that person is also tall, blond, and rail thin. That's right, folks, I have a friend who looks like Barbie! Literally, she does, and I mean that in a nice way. My friend is one of the smartest women I know, but she also is built like a blond bombshell Barbie!

The first time I flew in a plane with her was the first time I realized that strangers actually do put your luggage in the top bin for you. Well, I thought to myself, they do if they are male and see her. I thought at first it was an all-male thing, but we were in a restaurant and the female maître d'said there were no tables available for us. As disappointment set in, we decided to hang at the bar and wait to see if something became available. All of a sudden "Barbie" comes around the corner and says, "They have our table ready." What? Really? How does she do that? we were all thinking.

She's really amazing at getting what she wants. She has some amazing invisible superpower. She's always seen without even trying to be seen. I think that is a cool quality. She has taught me that even if it looks, feels, and seems unattainable, it never hurts to ask again. Also to always act with confidence in yourself, no matter the situation you are in, and the people around you will respond to it. Some days it's harder than others to live by this.

There are days I look in the mirror and see a pretty person. I also see some things I'd like to change. I have learned that I need to accept the good and the bad. I see a semifit person that would like to get stronger. I see bags under my eyes reminding me to get more sleep. I see lackluster skin that tells me to drink more water. I see all these things and wonder, How did I survive all those years and come out on the other side still seeing the rainbow? I have tried to instill in my daughters good self-esteem in themselves even though I don't always have it in myself. I believe strongly that self-esteem comes from within ourselves, but outside influences can play a major role, too. So although it has not always been easy, I think they have both grown into strong, confident women.

In reality, I realize I could be all kinds of crazy. Where does my sense of confidence come from? When did I realize I wanted to be okay? I like myself. I don't fool myself into thinking I am anywhere near "Barbie" potential, but I think maybe that simple fact that I am willing to pat myself on the back and let myself have down days and sleep to the middle of the day when I need to, allows me to say I'm okay. I made it. I know not everyone that has been in a terrible situation can say the same. I see with my own eyes how bad it can be and how hard life is. No matter how much I want to believe magic exists in the world, I know that magic only works if you believe.

I accept myself for who I am and the limitations I know I have. I could let those limitations be roadblocks in my life, but I know I will want to overcome them in some way. In the end, though, I will always be on my side. I get that lots of things have gone into making me who I am today. Even those eighteen years had a role to play. I accept the bad that has happened to me, and I don't slap myself down for the "what ifs" in my life. What if I had beaten myself up all those years in the backyard? What kind of person would I be now? Why didn't I beat myself up?

I think reading had a lot to do with it. I read a lot. Books on every subject I could get my hands on. Phillip had a lot of self-image and self-help books and stuff lying around from his time in prison, and I would read everything I could about positive affirmations and behavior. What we say to ourselves really matters.

Much more than I think we even realize. I saw a book recently meant to motivate people to exercise and eat right, but it was so full of rude, mean-spirited comments that I don't see how anyone could see past it to the real useful information it contained. How does it work to motivate by putting down? It doesn't in my book. For every negative thing I say to myself or that I hear (yep, I'm not perfect as you all might have thought!), I always try to say something positive instead. Like how could you eat that donut when you know we are trying to be low-carb! I can change that into Okay, we had a donut, let's stay on track from now till the end of the week. That always makes me feel better. Or I will look at a picture of myself and think, OMG, I have the biggest arms in town: they look like gigantic white ham hocks! I can turn that one into It's okay, I'm exercising and lifting weights. My arms are strong and full of muscle, girl! Or I could say, Next time I think I will wear a longer-sleeved dress for sure! Honestly, though, on those days I feel my heaviest, I look in the mirror and remember that I am healthy, active, and—best of all—happy to be able to be beautifully flawed and fancy free!

Most Embarrassing Moment

Horses have been a big part of my recovery and my new life. They have brought many moments of happiness, discovery, laughter, and most of all, they remind me that it's okay to look stupid sometimes, and though others might judge, a horse never will.

On one such occasion a horse named Velcro thought I needed a lesson in being seen, a little too much for my liking. Freesia and Velcro have been companion horses for years and like to go and do everything with each other. So when a friend was going to enter Freesia in a horse show, she encouraged me to try it out on Velcro.

At first I was reluctant to say yes. I have loved learning how to ride. I love riding for fun. I felt I had some skills in the arena, and my confidence had grown from where I started four years earlier, but the word *competition* sounded so scary, and one thing

I do not like to be is in the spotlight. My friend said it was a very small backyard horse competition, and since this would be my first one, I would be entered with riders of similar abilities. Well, I said yes, obviously, because I'm writing about it now, so we can skip forward a bit.

I practiced on Velcro at least twice a week and learned all that the judges required in a show like this. In my arena, I felt confident and we were working well together. Yes, we had days that Velcro thought I needed to be crushed into the fence a bit. Overall, though, I felt ready. I also watched my friend train. She is such a beautiful, quiet rider. I learn so much from just watching her ride and listening to our trainer instruct. When they are working in sync with each other it is a beautiful thing to behold.

Competition day arrived. I dressed in my horse show clothes. I didn't even know there was a certain type of shirt and pants one must wear to compete in a horse show, but there is. I had to wear a white polo-looking shirt and tan breeches. I should have had tall riding boots, too, but I could never find any that fit my calves, so I just went with my paddock boots and half chaps. Loading of the horses was our first order of business. Freesia was not a fan of the trailer and would sometimes protest.

It took all of us to convince her to get in the trailer, and by the time she finally went, yes, you guessed it, we were behind schedule. We had planned to get there an hour early to acclimate the horses to the new environment and ride them around a bit. Now, because of the late hour, that was not going to happen and we would be lucky if we made it with enough time to tack the horses up with their saddles and bridles before the show.

The morning was really foggy, and the place we needed to go

was way out in the country. The drive seemed to take forever. I was nervous and just wanted to get it over with. My division was up first.

We finally arrived, and I had to go enter my name. I used a fake name for my privacy issues, but now looking back, I'm so glad I did because can you imagine if this embarrassing moment made it on the ABC Channel 7 news! I know what you're thinking: we don't yet know what this oh so embarrassing moment is, Jaycee. Yes, so back to the story.

So I put in my name and received my number to be pinned to the back of my shirt. I was number 4 and felt ready for my first competition. As I looked into the arena, the other riders were in the ring already warming up. On closer inspection the riders appeared very young; in fact, they were young! OMG, I thought, my competition is eight-year-olds! How embarrassed I felt! (Wait for it: This is not the most embarrassing moment. This is just embarrassing.)

I was the oldest person in my division competing with kids. Well, I thought to myself, they will probably just think I am one of their kind because I'm short. For today I will be a tall kid!

I saddled up my horse and off we went into the arena. My mom was running late but said she would be there to watch me in time for the competition. I almost didn't want her to come now and see who I was riding against, but she was already on her way. It was hard to concentrate on what was being said over the loudspeaker. All thought of what I was supposed to be doing left my mind a blank. So I looked at what the others were doing and copied them.

Velcro and I set out on our journey around the edge of the

arena past the judges on the other side. I wondered, Do I have my correct diagonal? (It took me a long time to know when I wasn't on the right diagonal, which means I post up when my horse's outside leg comes back, which helps both us both stay comfortable and balanced.)

Velcro was looking everywhere at once. Her focus was not on me. She felt like she wanted to run and get ahead of the girl and her pony in front of us. I tried to hold back her power, which I could feel building, and I tried to soothe her with my voice. She started to prance in place and was really speeding up. Oh no, I thought, time to slow down now, girl! She felt really geared up, like she wanted to win the race she thought we were in.

I was sitting the trot, which is not what I was supposed to be doing at all. As we came around another corner, Velcro decided she had had enough and stopped dead in her tracks. I encouraged her with a squeeze to her sides, letting her know that this is not the time for stopping, but she didn't listen to the cue. Instead, she moved backward right into the tiny rider behind us and her pony! The girl had a pretty pink ribbon in her long braided hair and looked at me with daggers in her eyes! She seemed to be trying to say, Why can't you control your horse? I was so horrified.

I hear a voice over the loudspeaker. "Will competitor number four please restrain their horse?" "Number four, please leave the arena." I heard it over and over again from the loudspeaker. Who's number four? I wonder, then it dawns on me: it's me! They are asking for me to leave the arena. Everyone was looking at me! I wanted to check out and run away, but I couldn't. I had to get Velcro out of there, too. She refused to move a muscle. I really had to dig deep inside and remember all the advice Rebecca and horse trainer Margie had given me.

At that point, I looked up and saw my trainer entering the arena and walking straight for us. I wanted to exit the arena on my own to save some of my dignity, but I was also so very grateful for the escort. I saw then that my mom had arrived right in time for the brilliant show we had just put on. Brilliant not!

My hopes and dreams of the first-place ribbon were dashed. Then I remembered I entered this competition for fun, not ribbons. At the very least, I gave it a try and learned some valuable lessons. Like kids on their ponies take these shows very seriously and so do their parents. And I also learned that your friends will still love you and say you did a good job even when you do the walk of shame from the arena. I was officially part of the club and could honestly say I had entered my first horse competition.

Walk of shame.

Me on Velcro walking out of the arena with Margie.

First Christmas

I don't remember my very first Christmas, but I do still have an ornament that my mom kept that says "Jaycee's 1st Christmas." My mom even painted and glazed it herself. I remember when I was little, I used to like to go to the ceramics shop with her, and she would let me pick out a special piece that I could work on. I loved watching her work on the ones she was doing and turning them into magnets for our fridge. My favorite was an Oreo cookie that looked so real I could have eaten it. That magnet is still with us today.

That first Christmas for us in 2009 was really special. The girls did not believe in Santa Claus. For many reasons, it was not even possible to keep up the ruse of some make-believe man that came through the chimney to bring good boys and girls presents. For one thing, none of our tents or buildings had chimneys. Phillip was always so unpredictable that Christmas could always be canceled depending on his mood or whim.

I want to believe that the true meaning of Christmas is not receiving, but it is in the giving. I even tell my girls that. It's hard to believe in the magic and joy when there is so much filth and destruction on earth and you know that not everyone is having a merry day. Somehow, I still believe that we each hold the key to our own happiness, and you have to grab it where you can in whatever form it might take. It sometimes takes keen vision to spot that magic and, sadly, it goes unnoticed a lot of the time.

I'm not sure when I stopped believing in Santa. I guess maybe it was the year I was kidnapped, and the fact that he didn't show up with presents might have been my indicator. I'm not sure that I ever really stopped believing completely.

I know some wonder how I can be so happy and optimistic about everything when so much bad has happened. Rebecca and I explored this a lot in therapy. I worked hard in therapy with her to overcome any anger I felt toward Phillip and Nancy because, yes, it was there.

Rebecca always commented about my resiliency and ability to see the bright side of things even when faced with the ugly truth of life. She told me I reminded her of the boy in the story *The Polar Express*. This book is about a boy who travels to the North Pole to meet Santa Claus. Santa gives him one of the bells from his sleigh. Upon returning home, the boy discovers that he has lost the bell and becomes upset. Christmas morning, he opens a present and is surprised to find the silver bell from Santa inside. He holds it up and hears its musical jingle. His parents look disappointed and say that it's too bad it doesn't make a sound. They could not hear the bell, but the boy always could, even when he grew up.

The day Rebecca gave me the gift of the book, in it she wrote: "To the girl who will always hear the bell—regardless of what happens! With much respect and love, Rebecca." Secretly, I think Rebecca still hears the bell, too, and that's why she never gives up.

Sometimes I think I must sound like someone I am not. What I mean is I am not always filled with deep thoughts. I know presents are superficial, and there is much more to life, but I just love presents! I love presents any time of the year actually. I get so excited when I get a package from Diane von Fürstenberg with bright pink wrapping paper and her signature lips with a card that tells me she loves me. It makes me feel so special and unforgotten. It also reminds me that if I feel like this about someone sending me something, it's doubly important for me to try to remember to send the people I love something every year, too.

Chef Charles and I have been sending one of my favorites of his recipes to everyone we know for years now. It's called a sour cranberry tea cake. It has become part of Christmas. I usually send it out with a package containing homemade jams and cookies my mom and I make together. It is a package filled with extra love. I think that was a hard part about being gone all those years. All the people I loved had no way of knowing how much I missed them. When I returned, my mom, sister, and aunt Tina all taught me and the girls how to make little delicious peanut butter balls and Girl Scout Thin Mints that you make from Ritz crackers and melted peppermint chocolate that firms back up when it dries.

When I was first recovered, every new memory made with

jaycee dugard

family and friends was sacred. That first Christmas we still didn't
have a forever home, but we had each other. It actually kind of
snowed, well, more like hailed. We were living in an area where
that just is not supposed to happen. It's funny how I can almost
remember everything from that time, like the smells and the
sound. What we said to each other did not really stick, but everything else is still as plain as day. I think when I was kidnapped,
I closed off my senses like smell. That first Christmas back, my
mom gave us all Christmas jammies to wear to bed. Shayna had
found a stuffed cow ornament that had been donated to us and
it played "Moo-Moo-Moo . . . Mooooo-Mooo-Moo-Moo-Moo"
("Deck the halls with boughs of holly, fa-la-la-la . . . la-la-la"), and
she turned it on Christmas morning as we opened presents. That
first year I could not believe all the good wishes and generosity
of people. Phillip convinced me that I could never leave because
people would reject us and make my kids feel like outsiders to
the world. One of the things Nancy and he used to be sure we
never left was the fear of rejection and humiliation. They were
so wrong in every way! Most people have been more than kind.
I have never felt rejected. Sometimes a bit over-celebrated, but
never rejected.

That first year I received my first Droid smart phone and a
Nook. I was so excited. Having my own phone made me feel so
grown-up, and I couldn't wait to set it all up. Being held captive
for so long makes you feel like a child even at the then-ancient
age of twenty-nine. Every move I made had to be okayed by Phillip. Getting a phone for Christmas was significant on many lev-
els. It allowed me to communicate with whom I wanted when
I wanted, and at any point I could order a pizza. Believe me, at

that time that was a really new thing to be able to do. I mean, you could not exactly order pizza when you're held captive. My smart phone has gone through several upgrades now, and I have switched to an Apple iPhone. Actually, Apple everything. I know there is a lot of controversy out there about which is better, easier, smarter. What I love most about technology is that it allows me to keep in touch with family and friends.

My daughters are much older now; in fact, one is in college, and one is entering college soon. I am very proud of them both. They are both so important to me, and I am so proud of who they are growing up to be. You might wonder why not more of this book is about them since they are such a big part of my life. I have chosen it to be this way for the simple reason that I believe they deserve the right to their own stories. One day if they want to, they can write them their way. I've done my best to protect them over the years, just like any other mother would do for her kids.

Making new traditions is fun. For New Year's Day the past years we have been invited over by Chef Charles and Rebecca to make veggie animals. Yep, that's right: we make creatures out of stuff like fingerling potatoes, peppercorns, carrots, kale, broccoli, turnips, dried beans, and anything else that's left over from the garden. This tradition is so fun and makes you realize the new year is so full of fun and endless possibilities. It's grown over the years, too. It's always fun when someone new comes in and is skeptical of this weird project until their first creation, and then they get it. We had an amazing winter squash horse and carriage this year and a veggie man that we called "Papa New Guinea"! Try out having your own veggie party for all your friends and family. It's a fun way to start off the new year.

I once asked how this tradition started, expecting some deep meaning like the beginnings of the Thanksgiving holiday. Rebecca laughed and told me actually they developed it to give all of us a healthy way to celebrate the new year. She added that when we first came into Transitioning Families, there were times they struggled to come up with ideas to keep us all connecting. Not an easy task for a group who had not been with each other for eighteen years and who all shared different interests. Chef Charles had seen an artist named Alexander Calder who had made tiny circus animals out of wire, and he had thought, What a great idea. That first year I sat at a big table creating a family of vegetable animals with my sister, mother, daughters, and aunt Tina.

Me and Shayna.

First Christmas tree.

Veggie animals.

Our veggie animal creations, 2016.

That Time We Went to
See Garth in Ireland

So, do you remember that time you went somewhere to see a concert and then discovered when you are already there that said concert had been canceled? What do you do? Well, this happened. But, hey, I was in Ireland with amazing friends, and guess what we did. Made the most of it, that's what!

I had always wanted to travel to Ireland. I am an avid reader and love tales of magic and leprechauns and dreamy castles. I wanted to see it all. I needed to share this adventure and asked many friends and family if they would go. Unfortunately, not all could, but the ones who did were my oldest daughter, my aunt Tina, best friend Jessie, and our friend Kassel. Luckily, Rebecca was already planning to go, and she was taking her daughter, Chelsea, and son, Chris. We all planned to split the cost of a house for all of us to stay in together.

This would herald my first time traveling to another country, and so my very first passport stamp is Ireland!

You can see only so much of a whole country in a week. We let my aunt Tina be our event planner. She is the ultimate tourist. On the trip we took to New York, she taught us to walk across streets like the natives. Her motto: "Don't hesitate!" She's the best travel buddy to take trips with. When we were in Washington for the Hope Awards, she planned a Segway tour. Watching the video they make you watch is so unnerving and does not inspire confidence when you then have to go out and actually get on these contraptions after seeing all the things that can befall you on one! The group was scared, but Tina's enthusiasm infected us all, and we gave it a shot. Funniest thing ever! It's kind of like riding a horse. You need to bend your knees, and finding my balance was the key for me. My mom and Jane took to it like ducks to water. You would have thought they had been riding around on these things for years! Once we became more confident, we Segwayed around all the monuments.

In Dublin we rented a cute three-story house near Phoenix Park. It was right by a zoo and right down the street from the longest pub in Ireland called the Hole in the Wall. We toured local pubs, and I had my first Guinness. It was strong. I ended up liking the lighter beers.

On a trip out to see the Cliffs of Moher we had a very interesting bus driver. The Cliffs of Moher are on the southwestern edge of Ireland, so the ride was going to be an all-day adventure complete with lunch in a little town. We were all very excited. Our driver entertained us with stories of the towns we went through and the historical buildings along the way. I sat straight up in my seat. I didn't want to miss anything out the window. The day was beautiful and no rain in sight, which was unusual, we were told. The clouds look different in Ireland. They are bigger, fluffier, and whiter. His stories had a strange way of never ending and at the same time making little sense, and as the day wore on, I think we figured out why. The "street," if it could be called a street, was so narrow our bus was brushing things on either side, and when a car wanted to pass, we had to pull way over. When it was time to park at the Burren, it proved to be quite difficult for our driver to maneuver us around some of the rocks, and so he ended up scraping us by a big boulder and then backing us in a spot that only he knows why he chose. The Burren is a magical landscape that looks like you are on the surface of the moon. I could have sat there for hours, but all too quickly it was time to get back on.

We arrived at the Cliffs of Moher and explored the touristy spot. It was nice to stretch my legs and walk around a bit after being on the bus for so long. The cliffs are high above the ocean, and at places you can look down and see waves crashing below. I didn't get too close, though. I took a picture of a bee in a flower overlooking the cliff. Me and Jessie climbed to the top of the watchtower and pretended we were watching out for wayward ships. Tina and Kassel took pictures from down below, and when we joined the group again, the wind had picked up. Not just an ordinary wind; no, this wind was strong. If we had wings, it could have easily picked us up and carried us up and away, it was so strong. We put our arms and jackets out and leaned into the wind. My hair was blown completely back and the wind was literally holding me up, and if I turned my back to it, it pushed me. It was so cold, too. What a spectacular sight to see.

We stopped for lunch in a quaint little fishing village and much to my surprise, there was the cutest little bookstore complete with sign that read The Old Book Shop! This was my favorite moment in Ireland. I love old books. I hurried inside and rummaged through them all until I found one that looked like an old Irish fairy tale book. Before I left, I took one more look around and found a treasure. I randomly pulled out a book to inspect it and on the inside cover were handwritten musical notes! Wow, I wonder what this tune is and who wrote it. I bought that one, too, from the man napping in the corner and left the store feeling very happy. At the pub where we had lunch, my friend's son Chris sat drinking Guinness while reading James Joyce at the bar. A perfect sight. There is a code of honor there that I had not encountered before, living in America. After we ate, I learned that to pay you just had to go up to the bar and tell them what you ate, then they would tell you how much.

On the ride back to Dublin, our driver had to stop four times to use the bathroom. When he asked the bus for the fifth time if anyone needed to go, we all shouted no. We were all tired and just wanted to get back. We had left Dublin around eight that morning, and it was already approaching eight thirty at night. As we found ourselves once again pulling into a gas station, we were all a little irritated at the driver but forgave him because maybe he had a bladder problem. He started in on one of his stories that went nowhere again. His driving was a little more erratic at this point, and we had some narrow misses with some mailboxes. As we got on the only highway that Ireland had, we all sighed with relief because our journey with the driver was almost over. He interrupts himself midway through a story to ask once again if anyone needs to go to the bathroom. Again we all say no. After a few more minutes, we hear him loudly announce that he is sorry, folks, but his "kidney problems" are acting up, and he swerves over to the side of the highway and pees on the side of the road! I was laughing; some in the bus, however, were not. I couldn't blame them; it was strange. I wondered whether our driver had a wee bit of something in the front with him. I was so glad when we made it back in one piece. As we disembarked, he slurred, "Now, if you enjoyed this tour, please go to Trip Advisor and give me a good rating, will ya?" Um, no, probably not going to happen. I will always remember him and his "botatoe famin" stories and how he would say "however" every other sentence he said. He kept us very entertained for the whole trip.

I experienced so much on my trip to Ireland. I went bar hopping with Jessie, and we ended up talking to some local fishermen who were waiting for their wives to pick them up. They were good-natured but had very strong accents that, combined with all the pints they had obviously drunk, made them very hard to understand. They told us amazing stories and bought us a round of Guinness. I wasn't surprised when the bartender looked at me and said, "I'm going to assume you're of age." Yes, numb nuts, I'm over thirty! Gosh, will I ever look my age? I'm always told it's a good thing to look so young, but it's annoying at times. It was especially annoying in Ireland because the legal drinking age is eighteen. We listened to the Irish folk band playing, and I asked

Jessie which one she thought was cutest. She said the guy on the right, and I laughed. She didn't have her glasses on, or I'm sure she would have picked the one on the left!

The eight-hour time difference was hard to get used to, but there so much to do and see even without the concert. The locals were divided in their opinions on the concert being canceled. It was a big deal, and I bet Garth felt bad about having to cancel. That didn't stop us. What I wanted to see most was a castle. I ended up seeing a lot but only touring two. Malahide Castle was home to the Talbot family and dates back all the way to the twelfth century. Walking the halls, I felt what it must have been like to live in such an enormous structure. The living quarters were always upstairs because they were warmer. There is a beautiful tree you can see from almost every window of the castle. It is called a cedar of Lebanon and thought to be more than four hundred years old. I can imagine the countless kids that have played in its branches. I know I would have liked to.

The next castle was the Dublin Castle. This one was more modern or had been updated a lot more throughout the years. It was also really big. We did get to go underground and tour the oldest parts that still remained, so that was really cool. Kassel gave me a penny to make a wish on. I threw it into the old well. Malahide Castle was much more of what I thought of as a castle. Dublin was too modern for me.

Another fun memory was taking a horseback ride through the country with a guide. I had visions of riding a tall, leggy Irish warm blood, but in reality they gave me an Irish draft and gave my friend Jessie the leggy, elegant horse! Hey, the Irish draft and I do have a bit in common though; we are both tough and sturdy and very reliable. Plus, Jessie got a nip from her horse, so clearly I got the good one. We left from a historic monastery site. We saw Connemara ponies on the side of a lush green hill nibbling grass. Miles and miles of ferns grew in the forest we traveled through. Going on a gallop through the forest was so much fun, and my horse felt very safe. Our guide told us that the only predators were small foxes, but the mosquito population in some spots literally tried to eat us alive.

The scariest moment on the trip was when Tina got lost. We had split up to do some shopping and planned to meet back at a shop we all knew. It was the only day it decided to rain while we were there. It rained buckets on us. At the appointed hour, we all met up except no Tina! We waited for hours on that corner. It was so scary. I was really getting worried. Only one of us had a cell phone, and it wasn't Tina, so we couldn't call her. I thought something terrible had happened to her. Where was she? We decided two of us would take a cab back to the house and then call if Tina was there. We hoped she remembered the address to the house. I decided to stay, and I kept the cell phone with me. It was hard waiting and not knowing what to do. I was getting just a small taste of what my mom went through when I was missing all those years. Finally, the phone rang. I sighed a big sigh of relief when I heard Tina's voice on the phone saying she was okay and that when she couldn't find the street to meet at, she took a taxi back to the house. I was just happy she remembered the house address. I don't know what I would have done in the same situation.

On the way back, I experienced my first twelve-hour plane ride. It was one of the hardest things for me to do, but I managed to sleep most of the way back. When I wasn't sleeping, I was watching whatever movie they had on, which helped the time pass more quickly. It was still a very long time to be in a closed-in space. In the future, I would try to avoid long flights. It's a really great exercise if you are trying to improve your patience, though.

I will always remember so much about this trip and the amazing, nice people we met. I hope to return to Ireland one day and do an all-out horse trip!

Segways in Washington.

Blown away on the Cliffs of Moher.

Me and Jessie getting blown away on the Cliffs of Moher.

The Old Book Shop in Ireland.

Me and Jessie sharing a pint in an Ireland pub.

Me and Aunt Tina
in front of a castle
in Ireland.

Horseback ride
in Ireland.

Most Frustrating Moment

I take driving as a very serious privilege, not a right. So my first speeding ticket came quite by surprise. I was late for a board meeting, and isn't "late" when all your common sense goes out the window? I was so focused on getting to where I needed to be, I wasn't really paying attention to things like speed limits.

I had been through that particular stretch of town countless times and knew it went from 55 to 45 in the blink of an eye. That fact did not slow me down, and I heard a siren behind me. Still oblivious of my blunder, I thought the police officer only wished to pass me. To say I was surprised when he proceeded to follow me to the side of the road would have been an understatement.

Armpits filled with sweat in 0 point 2 seconds! I turned off the car and rolled down my driver's side window. I had to remind myself of what I had seen when people got pulled over on TV.

Always the officer would say, License and registration, please. So over and over in my head was that phrase: license and registration, license and registration. As I rummaged around trying to find what I needed, I thought, Oh my, who put all this crap in my glove compartment? Why can't I be more organized? It's funny the weird things that you think about when you're nervous. Finally, I found the documents and pulled out my license from my wallet. I sat patiently waiting for the officer that pulled me over.

I go over what I want to say, but I'm so nervous and afraid, I worry that nothing will come out right and he will think I'm insane or drunk or an idiot! I had fully expected him to be at my driver's door window, so when he did the safe thing (duh!) and came to talk to me from the passenger window, I jumped a mile in my seat and hit my head on the ceiling. He tapped on the window and I rolled it down. "Hello, ma'am, do you know how fast you were going?" he asks. I think to myself, Um, yep, way too fast apparently because I'm being pulled over.

To save myself from some embarrassing speech, I simply confess, yes, and I'm sorry. I really was sorry, sorrier for not thinking about this particular stretch of highway and being more present, but sorry nonetheless and just wanting this moment to be played in fast-forward mode. He says the famous line, "License and registration, ma'am," and I hand him the documents. I ask lamely if I have given him the right ones. He answers yes and then asks if I live here and I answer yes. He says then I need to get my address changed to my current one. I answer with a smile and say I like my privacy and I have had trouble with the media in the past so I don't want to get it changed for those reasons. I told him the chief of police knows me and approved. I admit I name-dropped the chief's name hoping by some miracle that this cop would say, Oh, you know the chief. I will just let you off with a warning. I had seen that happen before on TV. Real life is not TV, and of course that didn't happen. Instead, I hear him under his breath say, Yeah, lady, we all like our privacy. He looked at me like I was crazy, and I realized in that moment he had absolutely no idea who I was. Even looking at my license it had not registered. With such a unique name, I always feel like one gander and it's over, but apparently not with this guy. No, he just thinks I'm some lady who's really into herself and wants her "privacy" for some odd reason, which meant nothing to him.

He was just doing his job. He looked at me one more time, and as I flubbed around for what to say next, he walked back to his car. I'm not sure if he ever made the connection to my story, but he came back with my ticket for sure and told me to drive the speed limit from now on. Pulling away before him was so hard. I felt like everything I did was being scrutinized. Of course, he was probably on to his next thing, but I made sure I put on my blinker as I pulled out onto the highway and stayed at the exact speed limit all the way to the board meeting.

My excuse for being late was my first speeding ticket, and laughs and condolences were given and exchanged. It felt good to hear about their first speeding tickets, too, and I didn't feel like I had made a big mistake after that. I was just another human being in the world and allowed to make mistakes, too.

Journey to a New Land

When the opportunity to go to a place called Monkey River in Belize came up, I couldn't pass it up. It sounded so exotic and beautiful. A place with monkeys and beaches! Sign me up!

I learned about this trip from Rebecca. She and her husband, Chef Charles, were already planning to go, along with their daughter, Chelsea. Rebecca had known the organizer of the trip, Ted, from way back. Growing up, she had spent many summers with her family on an island off the coast of Maine called Isle au Haut. Ted was the local minister of the community and family friend. Although Ted had taken many volunteers to his adoptive town of Monkey River, this would be the first time she and her family came along.

When I learned more about the trip, I realized it wouldn't be a total vacation. From Ted I learned that Monkey River and its inhabitants were devastated by Hurricane Iris in 2001. Ted, a longtime fisherman, started the Monkey River Project to help rebuild this isolated community and also help educate fishermen about sustainable fishing practices. He organizes volunteers to go on these trips periodically throughout the year.

The thought of totally immersing myself in a culture was new to me, and the opportunity to help out was also appealing. I wanted to challenge myself. I had never been to a third world country before. This seemed like a really good opportunity.

I told some of my friends about the trip, but most couldn't get away from their busy lives. One friend though, Kassel, that I had met at Jessie's wedding in 2012, didn't want to miss out on this adventure.

Before making the final decision to go on this trip, it was important that I knew whether it would involve any religious preaching. I had had just about enough of preaching after years in the backyard with Phillip. I have true respect for people and their religious beliefs as long as they keep them to themselves or only share with those who ask. I learned that the trip would be nondenominational and nonreligious.

Although there would be some really fun and exciting aspects to this adventure, I also knew there would be manual labor involved. At first I thought Ted was looking for people with special skills. I've never really thought of myself as having any special talents, and I wasn't sure what I could contribute. I always wanted a special talent when I was little, a really cool one like being able to dance or blow bubbles out my nose! Despite my apparent lack of talent, I still wanted to go. I don't mind hard work, and I can hammer a nail. Plus, I couldn't pass up the chance to snorkel and see Mayan pyramids.

I feel very blessed for all that I have received and really wanted to give back to people less fortunate. The thought of going to a place where no one knew who I was or what I had been through was hard to pass up, too. In the past, a few organizations that had contacted me seemed interested in just using me as a poster child to advertise their cause. Having my own foundation keeps me pretty committed to my own cause. I just wanted to go to Monkey River to be another ordinary person helping out.

Since 2001, despite its remoteness, the village has continued to persevere. Even with constant besiegement from the ocean and its horrible storms. Their village was all but destroyed a week after 9/11 by a huge hurricane. Over a mile of their small beach was wiped out, which took away their tourist industry.

On this particular trip the goal was to help clean up the teacher's house, which would be a house the teacher could use to stay in. Monkey River has one elementary school that supports not only Monkey River but also the surrounding districts across the river. Each day schoolkids get "bussed" over in boats to go to school in the village. Older high schoolers from Monkey River ride over to get on a bus that takes them to the high school one hour away. Sometimes the road becomes flooded due to all the rain the area receives, which makes the trip even longer for them.

After disembarking from the plane at the Belize airport, I went through customs for the second time in my life. We were then met outside the airport by Ted and the other volunteers that would make up our group. Rebecca spotted Ted and introduced us to him, and he in return introduced us to the other volunteers: Tony, Jack, Rachel, Pete, and Walter. The plan was to journey from Belize City to Monkey Bay Wildlife Preserve for the night.

There was just one problem I saw. We had one van for eleven adults and their luggage. We needed some serious organizational skills to fit it all in. Each person had at least one suitcase and backpack! It was a very tight squeeze, but we made it fit.

Oh, and did I mention NO AIR CONDITIONER! It was around eighty-five degrees, and with all the people stuffed in the van, it felt much hotter! Plus, I get car sick. I had taken Dramamine for the plane ride, so I was okay. The road was very narrow, and although Ted was a good driver, we came very close to the passing trucks. Wow, thinking about it, I can't believe we made it in one piece!

Monkey Bay Wildlife Preserve is where researchers come from all over to study the ecosystem in Belize. Dinner that night was burritos with refried beans and fixings with sweet potato cakes for dessert along with tamarind and pineapple juice. The rooms were set up bunk-bed style. I slept like a rock, but others found it hard to sleep.

Since our trip to Ireland, Rebecca and I had started to work out religiously to get into better shape. So even though it was tempting to skip the exercise when on vacation, I didn't want to get flabby! I kept up my cardio with Rebecca with a run that first morning in Belize. We started down a dirt path from the preserve and ran down about a mile to the Sibun River, which connects to the local swimming hole. A little dirty for even my standards, LOL. We went back to the preserve for a shower. Did I mention there was no hot water? Make that the quickest shower in history.

We once again piled into the van for the Belize zoo. We saw jaguars, toucans, howler monkeys, ocelots, and many other native animals. Lunch was at the local farmers' market in the Belize capital of Belmopan. We chose a food stand called Deliah's.

After lunch we began the two-hour journey to Monkey River Village. The road was very bumpy all the way out to the inlet of Monkey River. Once we arrived, we took a small motorboat across the river to the town. It was such a beautiful view from the boat looking across to the town: palm trees swaying in the breeze, coconuts on the ground, people about their daily tasks. Lots of dogs roaming around as well.

During my stay in the village, I learned that the local dog population is a village unto itself with a social system unique to the setting. One dog in particular captured my heart. For some reason, this dog started following me around town. I have no idea why. I promise I gave him no treats. We had been warned that some of the dogs were not friendly and were encouraged not to engage with them. Rex, for reasons of his own, took a liking to me and wherever I went, he could be seen. He was a pit bull and, true to the stories, as sweet as sweet could be.

Rex always made me smile every time I would see him behind me. Quietly following me wherever I went. One day when Chelsea, Rebecca, and I decided to go for a swim, a funny thing happened with Rex. I walked out into the nice warm water. There was a very long stretch of shallow water due to beach erosion. I could walk a long way without being totally submerged in the water, which was nice because you could sit in the water and it made you feel like you were in a bathtub! As I walked farther out, all of a sudden I hear shouting behind me. I looked back and the group on the beach, watching out for sharks, was shouting at the dog that was paddling his way out to me. Rex decided that even water would not separate us. So sweet. When it was time to leave the town, it was hard saying good-bye to such a sweet dog. I hope he is still that sweet dog I remember. Unfortunately, half the dogs in the village do not get spayed or neutered. I know Rex had a very good owner that took really good care of him and his fellow dog mates.

About two hundred people live in Monkey River. We were greeted by Debra, the hotel owner. The "hotel" was really just a run-down two-story shack of a building. I really couldn't believe it was standing at all. In fact, some of the support beams looked very iffy and appeared to have massive termite damage. I know I lived in a tent, but it was never this bad. The people are very poor here.

As we explored the hotel, we found there was one bathroom downstairs and one upstairs. The toilet was hard to flush, and there was the biggest spider with the longest legs in history living in there. I hoped I didn't have to go at night! Two people per room. I bunked with Chelsea in a room upstairs. We also teamed up for the eating schedule. Two people per household in a rotating schedule, so we ate with one family breakfast, lunch, and dinner for two days and then switched to the next host family. Kassel was my dinner partner, and dinner the first night was with Cazerine. She made us stewed chicken, yellow rice, and salad. She was the teacher in Monkey River for sixteen years. She had six kids and eight grandchildren. We finished the night with a beer and sat by the beach with some of the group. The sound of the ocean was so relaxing.

One of the volunteers, Walter, was a doctor, and he wanted to get the clinic back up and running while we were there. There was no medical doctor on the inlet, so all serious cases had to be boated and bussed into the nearest town. We cleaned the clinic for two days. There was a two-foot termite nest in the back bathroom. Gross! Chelsea, Charles, and I swept and mopped the floors. Rebecca cleaned the toilet. Pete fixed lightbulbs. The clinic opened on Monday and stayed open the entire ten days we were there. The line of patients never ended. Makes me sad to think they have no access to a full-time doctor. Reminds me of how my kids grew up without a doctor, too, and how scared I would always be when one of them got sick.

Kassel, Chelsea, and I played soccer with some of the village kids. It was fun to just run around and play a game. I about laughed myself to death. Who knew it could be so fun just to kick a ball around with friends?

Kassel and I had lunch at Cazerine's where I tried fried snook for the first time! Not a fan. Thank goodness for the beans, broccoli, and cauliflower! After lunch, the kids took us down to the beach and we went swimming. We explored a ruin of an old house. I also saw the school for the first time that day.

I even had time for a nap that day, which was nice after the game of soccer. When I woke up, I went for a stroll down the beach to take some pictures. It then started raining, so I took shelter on a bench by Ivan's bar. The dogs know just where to lie to not get wet. Rain showers are very frequent there. Charles came to get coffee and sat for a while until the rain subsided.

Later that day, the supplies for the teacher's house came by boat. The group unloaded the supplies, and I helped take all the wood to the house for the project. We made a plan to start the next morning after breakfast.

Dinner that night was lobster fritters, rice, beans, salad, fried plantains, and banana bread for dessert. It was all really good, but the shells in the lobster fritters were hard to eat around.

It's impossible to sleep in on Monkey River. The roosters start crowing at 3:00 a.m. every day. Which gets the howler monkeys started, which makes the dogs bark. The mornings are not quiet and peaceful. But I was not there for relaxation, I was there for the new experience, and I was getting the whole shebang.

Every morning Rebecca and I would exercise in some way or another. We wanted to keep active even though it was tempting just to lie on the beach and relax. Some of the local ladies would come and watch us, and we asked them to join us. We formed what we called the Monkey River Exercise Crew. Soon more local ladies joined us each morning for an exercise routine. While there, we learned that the community had a serious issue of diabetes as the women were quite overweight. Many of them died young of diabetes. One young lady was shocked to hear Rebecca was fifty-three, stating that "she should be dead"! It was not the norm there to be over fifty and fit.

I learned a lot about the impact of poverty on food choices, even in a small tropical community. Many villagers used to be farmers, and fresh food was readily available and used. But then the banana plantations moved in and wiped out the local farmers, which left the community importing their food, most of it not fresh. Exercising takes some creativity on a small inlet of land. We used what was available, and coconuts became our weights.

Even though I am not religious, I thought it would be good to observe the local custom of attending church on Sunday. So after breakfast we all went to church, and Ted, the leader of our group, gave a very nice sermon and we sang songs together. It was actually a nice way to connect further with the community.

Later that day, I went fishing with Kassel, Tony, and some local boys and learned how to use a hook and line. It was fun to learn something new. I caught my first small little fish but let it go. We watched the Super Bowl before dinner and had a beer at Ivan's, where the locals hang out. It's kind of like a bar, store, and restaurant all in one location.

We went to a new house for dinner that night. Our hostess's name was Drina. On the last day she gave Kassel and me some homemade coconut oil. Drina cooked Kassel and me barracuda, black beans, and Johnny cakes. Not a fan of barracuda, but I ate half and Kassel ate the rest for me. We went back to the bar and watched a little more of the game, but I decided to go outside to get some fresh air and watch the sunset.

Breakfast was usually served at seven. After breakfast I usually went to Ivan's and had a cup of instant Starbucks mocha. I had brought the flavored coffee straws with me. Never leave home without your Starbucks!

Work on the teacher's house continued each day. We worked on removing the moldy, termite-ruined walls. All the walls needed to come down, actually. After that was done, Charles, Jack, Kassel, and Rachel sprayed for termites while Tony, Rebecca, Chelsea, and I went fishing. I caught another fish with just a line, bait, and hook. We stayed out for two and a half hours, and then I started to feel sick, so the boat dropped me, Chelsea, and Rebecca back at Monkey River while Tony went upriver to try to catch something bigger like a snook. Dinner that night was fried chicken, French fries, and tortillas. After dinner I would usually take a very fast shower (with cold water: yikes!).

One night the locals told us that it was a good night to watch for crocs in the river, so we went to the beach to try to spot one. I didn't see anything, but the moon was very full and the ocean looked beautiful.

On the sixth day, we put up the new walls for the teacher's house. I mostly nailed them with somebody holding the wall for me. After our day of work, we were treated to a lunch of fried chicken, French fries, and potato salad. After lunch we went back to work and then cooled off with a swim in the ocean.

That night dinner was at Ivan's. He made us spaghetti and garlic rock shrimp. It was very yummy. It was the first time Kassel didn't get any of my fish; he was very disappointed. For dessert, Ivan made us a cake with caramel sauce. The others came in after they were done with their dinners and wanted to mooch off our cake!

The next day we left bright and early at six for a cruise up the river to the jungle. Beautiful views surrounded us as we coasted down the river in a motorboat. Our guide was Darryl, and he was the dad of Malverie, one of the local ladies in town we had met and befriended. Malverie makes jewelry to sell at the local shop, and she let us pick a special piece to take back with us; I picked one with a fish. Seemed appropriate to remember this trip by.

Along the river, Darryl pointed out several birds, and we caught a glimpse of a croc for a second. We even saw tiny bats that were hanging onto a rotten tree trunk that was sticking out of the water. Darryl pointed out the male in the center of the group of six. He was easy to spot because he was the smallest one.

Next he pointed out a very tall tree that on first inspection looked like it had dried leaves hanging from it. In fact, those dried leaves were nests! There were hundreds on that one tree alone. Darryl told us that the tree was rare, and that particular species liked to make their nests on it.

After about four more miles, we pulled ashore and took to the jungle for a stroll. We made sure to spray ourselves from head to toe with mosquito repellent. In some places you could see swarms of mosquitoes just waiting to suck our blood! Darryl pointed out many native trees and told us of their usefulness. One tree's bark was used for snakebites.

At one point, our guide left us in a clearing to go find howler monkeys for us to see. I have to admit it was a little scary being left alone in the middle of the jungle. We were all a little jumpy. Chef Charles kept wandering off exploring, and we would all shout at him to stay together! Finally, Darryl, our guide, came back and led us to where a group of howler monkeys were gathered together. It took awhile because he said the full moon and tide made them sleep in. The monkeys were very high up in the trees and hard to spot at first. We had been warned that they could decide to pee on us, too, so best to keep alert. It was a group of four, and one had a baby on its back. They did some howling for us and put on quite the show. Luckily, they didn't pee on us. The return trip back to Monkey River was fun because the boat went fast.

We were all pretty hungry by the time we returned. We had lunch at Ivan's, and it was onion and chicken soup with coconut rice and very delicious. We worked on the ceiling of the teacher's house after lunch and finished about half of it before Tony, Jack, and Pete went fishing. Some of us stayed to clean up what we could, and a local man came over and brought us fresh young coconuts to drink. Yum. Fresh coconuts are so delicious when you are hot and sweaty. I remember the day was so humid, and the coconuts were the perfect thing to cool us off.

Strolling was fun to do in the village because it was nearly impossible to get lost. There are only three or four streets left in town, and there are absolutely no cars. There used to be more streets, I was told, but they were washed away with the beach. We watched the local woodworker carve beautiful bowls. It was amazing how he carves these beautiful bowls from the trunk of a specific tree that he hunts for days.

What I liked about Monkey River and what really surprised me was the kids and how inquisitive and thankful they were. Ordinary things that we take for granted mean the world to them. They treasured the art supplies and games we brought them. It was fun to watch them play all around the village. With there being no cars around, it was especially safe for them to ride their bikes everywhere. With all the bad things I have seen in the world and even knowing the poverty level there is so high, it refreshes me to see these kids just being kids. I know they have it bad, but they are very resilient.

I also loved to walk around and look at the different types of houses that were built there. Each house is built on stilts so they are above the water. Some are small and some are larger. They are all very colorful, and each reflects the personality of its inhabitants, I think.

One day I took a walk with Rachel over to a place the locals call Tiger Beach. Kassel and Hector, a local boy he had befriended, were already there fishing. He also had eight other boys that had tagged along. It was very funny to see. Rachel and I walked all the way to the oldest tree in the village, which was right by the ocean and half destroyed. Sad to see that this once-proud tree was home to countless termites now and slowly dying.

The next day we went snorkeling. It was my first time, and I was so excited to learn how. Rebecca, Kassel, Chelsea, and I rented a boat and guide, and he boated us out to one of the many surrounding keys. We had missed exercise class that day, but much to our surprise, a local named Cyndy said she would conduct the class for us. Snorkeling was so much fun but much harder than I anticipated. I found it hard to breathe through the snorkel but eventually kind of got the hang of it. I also learned that day I am not a great swimmer. Much to my embarrassment, I had to use the life jacket to stay afloat and not feel like I was sinking. I couldn't open my eyes because the sun was so bright and my eyes are very sensitive to light, and the sunscreen was stinging them, too. Our guide took pity on me and tossed me a towel to rub my eyes, and that felt better. I wish I knew how to put on sunscreen without it getting in my eyes. I don't think snorkeling will be a career choice for me in the future. The life jacket made me look like a nerd, but it made me feel safer.

Being out in the middle of the ocean is terrifying and thrilling all at the same time. Our guide, who had only one arm, by the way, was way cool! He was the best swimmer I had ever seen. He dived down to the bottom of the reef and pointed out a large lobster hiding in a rock. He also spotted a small shark that darted out so fast it was all a blur to me. Diving was hard work and really works up an appetite. We decided to find a nice spot for a picnic.

The key that we landed on was beautiful and loaded with hermit crabs. I was so excited to take pictures of them and send them to my daughter, who used to have her own hermit crabs. She would have been so excited to see this village of them. We ate lunch on the beach, and I fed some of my biscuit to the hermit crab that was scuttling around me. Our guide shouted to us to come over to the boat and said he had spotted a manta ray. We piled in the boat and floated over the area and then we saw it, too. A pale shape in the water that just glided over the surface. Beautiful. On the return trip we went through the mangroves and tried to spot manatees but didn't see any. I hope to see some next time.

Dinner that night was at the household of a local lady named Enid. We were served fish backbone and rice and beans. Not a big fan of fish, so this was a tough dinner for me to eat. It's hard not to be thankful for what you are given because the locals have so little.

After our morning exercise on our ninth day, we learned that Debra, the owner of the hotel we were staying at, was planning a trip into the nearest town. After weeks without a good latte and fresh veggies, several in our group wanted to go, including me!

After we finished working on the teacher's house and it was finally done (it felt so good to have it accomplished!), we set off on a journey to a town across the river called Placencia. Once there, our first order of business was to find the local coffee shop. I had my first iced caramel macchiato in a week. It was no Starbucks but very delicious anyway. We shopped around and had lunch at a Thai restaurant. The town was not very big, but compared to Monkey River, it was huge. You could buy fresh veggies, which is what Charles did for the party the village was giving us that night. After a few hours, we returned to Monkey River and relaxed the rest of the day.

That night we all went to Ivan's, where there was some interesting food served and dancing for those that wanted to. I was too embarrassed to dance in front of half the town, so I just watched with Chelsea. I tried rice wine for the first time and decided I didn't care for it too much. I sat outside and watched the kids play with paper airplanes. It was nice to see them having so much fun. It was a fun party and a nice way to end our trip. The next day, we left for Belize City. Saying good-bye to everyone was really hard. I hope to return to the tiny village one day.

Along the road, we stopped to see the local pyramids. They were different than what I imagined the Egyptian pyramids to be. Beautiful in their own way, though. We climbed around on them, and you could go to the top of some of them. Being in a place where so much history had taken place was a weird feeling. Not sure how to describe it. Eerie in a way.

We made it to Belize City in the afternoon. We all stayed at a hotel and went to dinner. We were told it was not safe to roam the city past dark. I had my first hot shower in over a week in that hotel. It felt incredible. I forget how much I take for granted nowadays. The next day we got on a plane for our six-hour plane ride home.

I will always remember my trip to Monkey River. The people there really inspire me with their unstoppable spirits. They want their community to continue and thrive, and I can see why. I met some incredible new friends on this journey, and I will always look fondly on my time there and respect the many lessons learned from its inhabitants.

Monkey River trip.

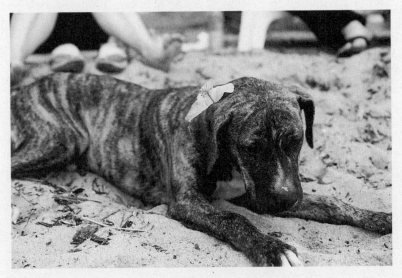

Rex from Monkey River.

Me putting a flower on Rex.

Me reading with a girl and ever-faithful Rex by our side.

Hotel we stayed in on Monkey River.

Cleaning the clinic.

Working on the teacher's house in Monkey River.

Me and Rebecca hammering the walls in Monkey River.

During clean-up on the teacher's house in Monkey River.

Me doing yoga on one of the keys in Belize.

Me, Rebecca, and Kassel in the Belize jungle.

Me doing more yoga in the jungle of Belize.

Me, Rebecca, and Kassel enjoying fresh young coconuts after working on the teacher's house.

Snorkeling in Belize.

Snorkeling with life preserver.

Snorkeling with life preserver and taking pictures underwater.

Me enjoying my first caramel macchiato in Belize.

Two Psychologists and a Survivor
Walk into a Bar . . .

You should never leave home without your therapist!
That's why I sometimes travel with two!

This has become the funny joke I use when I travel with Rebecca and Abigail. I first met Abigail around the fall of 2014. She had come to meet Dr. Bailey and help out with a high-conflict-divorce family that Transitioning Families was treating.

During that visit, I learned we had a mutual interest in seeing Stockholm syndrome deleted from the public's eye. This had become an important issue for me, because to me the label of having Stockholm syndrome was degrading. I wanted to see a change in how the public saw those who had been through something like I had.

Because of Abigail's background in writing academic papers, Rebecca and I both saw the opportunity to turn our dream of a paper on this subject into reality.

To date, we have spoken at Harvard's grand rounds in

Boston . . . for some reason I always want to call that Ground Round! Being asked to present at Harvard was incredible. I thought I would feel really intimidated being in such a prestigious school and me not even going to high school. I thought I would feel stupid. However, the people we presented to were all very welcoming. Even though I was nervous as heck, we ended up having a lively discussion of Stockholm and its many downfalls. As a special gift, they gave us fleece Harvard jackets. I wore mine the whole day and pretended I had actually gone to Harvard!

We also spoke at a conference at Yale University and at the International Society for Traumatic Stress Studies (ISTSS) in New Orleans. We had a very prominent gentleman come up to us after our presentation and say he would never again use the term. High fives all around, ladies! We have had tons of fun traveling together and making fun memories.

New Orleans was a lot of fun. I thought it would be hard to go to a place that had been so devastated by Hurricane Katrina. But I loved it. The paper we presented together at the International Society for Traumatic Stress Studies was well received, and many thanked us for bringing this topic to the forefront.

That night we walked around the French Quarter, and Rebecca bought us each a T-shirt that represented us. Abigail got one that had a bedazzled shoe on it representing her love of designer shoes; she loves her Jimmy Choos! I got one with a knight on his horse because she knows I love horses and stories about medieval stuff. Rebecca's was a jeweled Mardi Gras mask, which I think reflected her love of dancing and her free spirit.

On the street corners were a lot of musicians. One duo captured our attention. Two ladies played a violin and a guitar, and they sounded like heaven. It was truly beautiful music. I couldn't believe they were not famous and were just playing on this street corner like this, in the hopes they would make enough money to live on one more day. They were so good, I had tears in my eyes. In fact, we all did.

A little about my friend Abigail. She is tall and blond and beautiful and, to my utter delight, sings like an eighty-year-old soprano! It's the best thing ever because she knows all the songs by Lil Wayne and Drake and oldies but goodies, too. When she sings them in her high granny voice, it can make even the grumpiest person laugh; I know I sure do! Perhaps that's why we like her and the only reason we keep her around!

She also loves Starbucks and has a beautiful greyhound named Cobblepot. When she first introduced us to her dog, I immediately had a vision of *Lady and the Tramp* and that scene in the park when everybody is walking their dogs and all the owners look like their dogs—she's one of them. Long legs and built just like her greyhound!

During a trip to Washington for NCMEC's Hope Awards, we all went for a private tour of Mount Vernon. A funny thing happened when we went over to where George and Martha were buried. I don't always pronounce things right, like my "wolf" sounds like "woof," and I was once caught pronouncing "tutorials" like "toot-uh-rolls." Another two words that get me all befuddled are "reef" and "wreath." Although I would like to say I know the difference, these words can sometimes come out of my mouth as the same. Rebecca always catches me on this, and we laugh hysterically about it. She's lucky I have a good sense of humor! On this day at Mount Vernon our friend had set it up for us to go into the tomb of George and Martha and place a wreath in honor of the occasion. When the wreath was presented to us, I couldn't help but think, Thank goodness, I don't have to give a speech about placing the wreath! Because I would surely say "reef"! That turned out to be a special and poignant moment for us and cemented our friendship. We came out feeling a strong sense of camaraderie. It was a moment I will never forget.

During our presentations of our critique of Stockholm syndrome, Abigail always keeps us grounded. I always get nervous and I rely on Rebecca and Abigail to get us through the technical background of Stockholm, and then we field questions about how it relates to me and my story. I always like to start out with the obvious: "I WAS NOT, I AM NOT, I WAS NEVER IN LOVE WITH MY CAPTOR!" Nor did I want to spend eighteen years of my life as a captive. That's more time than I had been alive, and today that is more time than I have been free.

During our presentation at Yale University, a lady with what looked like a small furry hedgehog on her head (which turned out to be just her questionably fashionable hat) posed this question: "Jaycee, what do you do for yourself?" The question was so unrelated to the topic that I wasn't sure how to answer. I ended up saying, "I do all of this for me. I started the JAYC Foundation for me. I wanted to give back to other families what I had been given. I was doing this talk because it was something I was passionate speaking out about. I do all this because I have hope that life does not end when you are kidnapped or raped or abused. I believe life goes on and all that you can endure can be channeled into positive things for others to learn and grow from."

After she asked me the same question two or three more

times in different ways, I could not help but wonder if maybe the hedgehog on her head was blocking her ears and she could not hear me. She did not seem to accept my answer, because later she approached me in a restaurant, this time without the creature on her head, and asked me the same thing again. I think sometimes people ask questions, but they have already formed the answer in their heads and cannot hear anything else.

Bear with me if you think I am belaboring the issue of Stockholm syndrome, but it's really the first time I have been really passionate about an issue. I am usually very neutral about things and can see both sides of an argument. This is different. There is no right side. It's wrong, and the label can be very damaging to the mental health of the victim being labeled. I have even talked briefly to Gina and Amanda from the Cleveland case when we all attended NCMEC's 2015 Hope Awards, and they believe it to be a misleading, degrading label for them as well. It seems to be a common complaint of many survivors.

When my two daughters and I were rescued in 2009, the news was covering my story heavily and I had no desire to watch any of it. I was living it. I was so happy to be reunited with my mom and family that it really wasn't on my radar to be offended at the time.

I realized later that I had been labeled as the "girl with Stockholm" and, honestly, it was very horrible hearing that. Not to mention the impact of family members thinking I had Stockholm syndrome. Once you hear something like that, it's hard to think it's anything else. That's one reason why this label is so damaging: because it gives an "explanation" for something that nobody but the victim truly understands and puts a nice, tidy bow on it for everyone else! Like all that I had survived and endured was being pushed down into two words. It makes all I went through seem insignificant and boils it down to "You loved your captor, therefore, you never wanted to be free" or somehow you were stupid enough to confuse abuse with love. Bullshit! You can't take something that happened in the '70s and pin the rap on all of us that come after. The incident that gave us that name was a very different hostage situation. But for some reason the news and media still like to use the term. It's used in TV shows and books all the time.

Phillip was good at making me feel sorry for him. He was a seasoned manipulator. I was a naïve girl. Phillip did not want to see me cry. He said it made him feel bad. I was alone. Completely. Years passed—years of abuse physically, verbally, and emotionally. I adapted to survive. We all can learn to adapt to survive. It's in our genes.

When I was little and lived with my grandma and grandpa in Garden Grove, we used to watch nature programs together. Thinking back on those shows, the interactions between predator and prey made me think about me and how I survived with a predator all those years. I began to see how I would use some of the techniques in those programs on Phillip and Nancy just by instinct. A friend of mine wrote a book on a subject that seemed to confirm a lot of what I already knew. It's called *The Power of the Herd* and combines my love of horses and my favorite subject: understanding power dynamics.

If I was prey, how did I survive so long in such a predator-dominated situation? Shouldn't I be dead? Not only did I survive but my kids did as well. I feel shivers run up and down my spine thinking about that and remembering the way my stomach would hurt every time I would see him. Look how easily our lives could have been cut short.

When you are captive you don't really spend time asking yourself why. Most of my energy was spent on surviving and protecting my girls. Protection meant diffusing his anger and trying hard to outfox both Nancy's and Phillip's manipulations. My terror ran deep. That kind of fear lives deep and it's hard to describe. I didn't feel it all the time, but it was there living inside and it kept me alive.

The predator in nature is ruled by needs and the pressure of survival. While the prey in nature is focused on survival first and basic needs second. When presenting our critique of Stockholm syndrome, we use a video to demonstrate. It starts out with an impala running for its life from a cheetah. You see the cheetah outrun the impala and grab it by the neck. The impala goes limp and the cheetah drags it away. The cheetah is exhausted by the run and thinks its prey is dead. Another predator comes along, a hyena. The cheetah is so tired it cannot protect its meal from the other predator and reluctantly leaves the scene. The next scene is the hyena walking over to the dead impala, but just as the hyena is about to sink her teeth into the prey, the impala whips up and darts away. We use this video because it is such a great example of prey versus predator and how the prey had to think like a predator in order to survive. In this case, the impala knew what the predator wanted—its death—and acted like it was dead to get away later and win another day.

Predators in our human world prey on the weak and the strong; to them there is no distinction. Phillip and Nancy both felt very much like predators to me. They stalked me up the hill I was walking on that fateful day in June. Had they seen me before? Did they see me at the flea market the day before, like some people speculate? They used their car as a weapon, using it to cut off any hope of an exit I had. He used his sharp teeth of a stun gun to take me to the ground. I was his helpless, weak prey that he dragged back to his cave for his consumption just as a predator would do. But I was cunning like the impala and eventually got my freedom.

There are days I think about all these issues and try to make sense of all that happened. I learned early on not to take what happened to me personally. It was not like I or my family ever deserved what happened. Maybe that's how to keep yourself sane after bad things: don't blame yourself. If I had blamed me, I am not sure I would have fared so well. It's important to take care of yourself first so that you can be there for others.

I know now that slowly but surely I discovered that I didn't feel like prey anymore. I didn't feel like a predator either. Although I had by this time spent so many hours with a predator that I was beginning perhaps to think like one to protect myself. I was watchful, observant, and cunning. Cunning, you ask? Yes, in my little world that Phillip had forced upon me I felt like a fox! Foxes are predators for sure, stalking prey. They are built for it with the right tools, but the fox is also hunted by those predators bigger than he.

So was the fox predator or prey? He is both! He is the in-between. I am the in-between. I knew I had not become this creature overnight. It was created inside me with perceived little victories. Little things that you would think are nothing, but to me they all felt like I was taking something back for myself. With each new freedom I gained throughout the years came personal growth and a better understanding of my captor, my known predator. I learned early on to watch for cues to his moods and adapt to those moods and flow with them to stay alive. I could almost anticipate his moods and emotions.

I share this now because I want people to understand what goes on when you are in the presence of crazy. It might look like intimacy from the outside, but don't confuse survival for true connection. So much was invested in keeping up with his thoughts and feelings that it took a toll on my own. I lost myself in all the complexity of the situation and have since my release been slowly building myself back up. I think we all have to do this process of self-discovery throughout our lives. We get so wrapped up in other people and their lives that we forget what is best for self. In my past that is what worked for me, but now that I'm safe, there needs to be a balance of self and then others. It shouldn't be others and then self. Self should come first, I think, even above kids because if you are not the best person you can be, how can you expect your kids to be?

Rebecca has been an amazing therapist to me, and now I count her as one of my friends and mentors. I sometimes wonder what if she had said to me in the beginning of treatment, "Jaycee, you are suffering from Stockholm syndrome." Would I have believed her? At the least it would have limited my recovery. Would I have questioned her diagnosis? She taught me that it's so important not to label people. I truly believe it would not have helped me but, rather, hindered me. I like to think I would have had the wherewithal to say, "Hey, stop saying that. No, I don't have

Stockholm syndrome." Now on the other hand, if Rebecca had said to me, which she did, "You adapted to survive. You did what you had to do and at times you make the best of what life hands you." This is a positive statement, and victims need positivity in their life, not hindering labels.

Okay, I will get off my soapbox now, but don't let me catch you or anyone else using the term Stockholm syndrome again. It feels so nice now to shout what I believe out loud. No one will tell me again what to say or not say. Okay, maybe they can tell me, but I won't listen. I choose to keep my life filled with people who want to hear what I have to say. They don't mind when I speak up.

The other day I was out with a friend, and the waitress brought me my soup. When I tasted it, it tasted like burnt socks with maybe a touch of my hated cilantro. At first I thought, Just eat it and keep your opinions to yourself. But you know what? As soon as the waiter came over, it just popped out of my mouth. I said, "Excuse me, but could you bring me the other soup? This soup tastes strange." It just came out just like that. My friend laughed as the waiter walked away. She said that she never ex-pected to see me speak up like that. Now, it seems silly—like why wouldn't you send soup back if it tastes gross?—but guess what. There was a time I never would have done that.

Me, Abigail, and Rebecca showing off our shirts in New Orleans.

Me, Abigail, and Rebecca sharing a moment in
George and Martha Washington's tomb.

Hope Is a Four-Letter Word

Hope is the thing with feathers that perches in the soul, and sings the tunes without the words and never stops at all.
—Emily Dickinson

Few things in life say love more than a "death by chocolate" cake. My mom happens to make a delicious one, and it's what I ask for every birthday we have been back together.

I think my mom is one of the bravest people I know. I don't know if I could have retained so much hope after eighteen years of waiting for my daughter to return to me. But that is exactly what my mom did. She told me about how she would talk to me throughout the years on nights with a full moon and tell me all about her day. I like to believe that I felt this love and it gave me the strength I needed to endure each day on my own without her much-needed guidance.

Since my miraculous return and the introduction to her new granddaughters, whom she had no hesitation in accepting, my mom has sacrificed much of her life to us. Although she would never say that, she has because that's the kind of person she is. She splits her time and energy to be with both me and my little sister Shayna.

Being in my thirties living with Mom has not always been easy for either of us. I'm not the same eleven-year-old I was when I was taken. She has always let me express myself and accepted that I'm not a kid anymore, even though I know she still worries every time I leave the house. Some memories even time cannot erase completely.

We have both worked really hard in therapy on ourselves and with each other. We have both shared many stories and memories, and she was so proud of how I raised the girls in the backyard. I think learning about each other has helped with accepting who we are now as opposed to who we used to be. My mom has shared some of her awful dreams she endured while I was missing. She told me one that happened in 1992; it went like this:

She was very busy in the kitchen at the house we had lived in in Tahoe. The lighting was very dim and dark. She was worrying and searching for something, trying to find something, going through cupboards and shelves, tearing out stuff, making a mess trying to find something. Then in I walked through the front door, and she could feel it was warm outside. In the dream, I was tapping her on the shoulder, trying to get her attention, and I said, "Mom, can I have a drink of water?" She was preoccupied, frantically searching for something, not realizing I was home, and she started to say "No, Jaycee, I'm busy, I'm looking for something" and then she suddenly realized I was what she was looking for and all she could do was hold me and cry. "You're home!" She says she woke up crying and clinging to her pillow, because I really wasn't.

I cannot even fathom the torment of dreams such as this, and she had them for all the years I was missing!

I have always known I am special in my mom's eyes; she always called me her number one. During therapy it helped to be reminded of her love for me, and it also helped to know she did all she could to find me. At times I lost hope of ever being rescued and found. I thought I would rot in that backyard and nobody really would ever care or even remember me. I told my mom my fear of being forgotten, and she hugged me and said, "Never! Never ever, Jayce. I looked my hardest for you and I never doubted for a minute that we would one day be together again." And we are!

My mom also told me about the garden that was planted for me in Tahoe and the memorial rock. Ten years after I was taken from that street in Tahoe, my mom wrote this:

Jaycee's Rock

There is a rock, quite steadfast by nature, located in a small town nearly five hundred miles from here. A single spruce grows next to the rock, reaching up to touch the ostentatious sky. The rock and the spruce are like many others in this quaint, little town; yet they are quite unique in my mind. Nearly eight years ago, these two were placed in this spot. Why? It is here that I go to remember the good times, mourn my loss, and renew my spirit. As I add to the flowers surrounding this sanctuary,

I remember a little girl who loved nature. My fingers dig into the rich, dark soil, and I feel her warmth radiating throughout me. My tears mix with the water that I sprinkle upon these blossoms. They are a reminder to me, as well as others, of a lively and cheerful little girl, my little girl, my baby. Just like this rock, my love for Jaycee remains steadfast and solid. Some say that as time passes, memories lose their sharp focus. The growing spruce is a reminder of time passing and also of something that will not die as long as it is nourished. The rock withstands the elements of time and so will she if only in my mind.

Since my return we have had many fun adventures together, building new memories and reliving old ones. She took me by the old house we lived in with my grandma and grandpa. I was amazed at how much smaller the property looks now than when I was little. I learned my mom has a terrible fear of water, but when I asked her to go on a kayaking trip down the Rogue River with Jessie and her family, she agreed even though she was afraid. This trip ended up being really fun for both of us. She stayed on one of the bigger boats and loved to soak up the sun each day, but on the last day she got in one of the little kayaks and realized it wasn't as scary as she thought it would be. That's the strength and courage my mom has in all things.

My mom is a fabulous designer and fixer-upper. She has put her talents to good use and helped with making our JAYC Foundation house feel homey and inviting for the families that come for reunification therapy. She also helps Chef Charles with food prep and planning.

I can honestly say I know my mom better now than I did when I was younger. Even though I loved my mom dearly when I was little, I love her so much more now. Age makes you appreciate people in your life with so much more than you could ever give them as a kid.

Me and Mom.

Me and Mom.

Mom baking me a cake.

Lil Sis

There were so many days in my sister's life that I wanted to be there for. In fact, I should have been there. I would have if two psychopaths hadn't decided that their lives were far more important than mine or my family's. I could only imagine what her birthday parties were like, what she wore to her first prom. I would have liked to have been there for all the moments of her life. I think I would have made a really good big sister. Despite not growing up together, I think we have a lot in common. One time she texted me a picture of the color she painted her nails, and I sent her an "LOL . . . me too" text. I had just had mine painted the same shade of purple. What are the odds we would both pick that color for our nails in the same week? We also share the same sense of humor and laugh at the same jokes.

So you can imagine how happy I was when she asked me to

come to her wedding. That's right: I was the happiest girl alive! It was going to be small, she said. Just me, our mom, and her husband-to-be's dad and stepmom.

My mom renewed her ordination so she could marry them. She also hand made Shayna's dress from a pattern that my sister loved. We went out hunting for the perfect spot the day before. Finally found one by a little lake. Later that day we went to this drive-through animal park. It was so fun feeding the animals straight out of the window. An ostrich got a little too friendly for my mom's liking, but Shayna and I thought it was hilarious as the giant bird tried to stick his long neck in the car to get at Mom's goodies. That was the first time I had been through a zoo like that. I loved how all the animals were basically free to roam around. There were bison, emu, sheep, zebra, deer, elk, and so much more. That was a fun day, and it just got better when Garrett took us to the best rib joint in town.

The morning of the big day I remember thinking, Gosh, look how beautiful my little sister looks. She's the only person I know who can look this good so early in the morning. How amazing this moment is for me to be here and witness her special day with the man she loves and who obviously loves her, too. The morning was foggy and chilly, but the setting turned out to be so perfect. The water was so calm and shining and reflective in the morning light. Steam was rising from the lake. There was an egret perching on the shore opposite where we were. As we pulled up, there was a police cruiser by the boat dock. I almost thought he was going to ask us to leave, but he just sat there eating his breakfast and didn't seem to be interested in what we were doing. Mom conducted the ceremony down by the beach. I tried to keep the tears of joy from overflowing, but I admit some leaked out. It was a short but sweet ceremony and before you knew it we were off to breakfast. My heart felt full. It was so nice to be part of a shared memory for a change.

A few months later they visited, and we had a fabulous, rocking party at my barn. Complete with a band and moonshine! The band was really cool because it was formed by a friend that's a real judge and his court staff. The band was called Courtin' Disaster and they played really awesome country songs. I've always been too shy to dance in public, and although I was surrounded by friends and family, I still felt that way when it came to dancing. I really wanted to dance, though, and we had an awesome live band. My friend taught me the secret of dancing. She said I needed to "crack the cage" and demonstrated what she meant. She said if you let the bottom part do the movin', the top part can just hang out and be cool. For some reason this made so much sense to me and I had no problem dancing the night away with everyone in my cool cowgirl boots complete with pink flowers on them. We had the whole event catered with delicious barbecue ribs, chicken, and baked beans and veggie burgers for vegetarians like my daughters. The whole night was a blast and a fun way to kick off their married life together.

I know it's okay to feel resentment and anger over the past. The key for me is moving past all that and living in the here and now. New moments and finding the joy in them is what makes me stronger every day, and a little help from family and friends never hurts, too.

Since the start of the foundation, Shayna and Garrett have been lifesavers. When we first came up with the idea to sell pinecone necklaces to raise money for the JAYC Foundation, I thought it would be easy to package them and ship them out. Well, thanks to the many orders we received—over 10,000, from all over the country—that turned out to be a daunting job. The necklaces came all tangled together and it was so hard to untangle them to be able to put the pinecone charm on.

I should have listened to my friend when asked how I would handle the orders that would come in, but I didn't think that far ahead. I just have the ideas, people. I didn't really have the ability to see beyond that and plan these things out. I think I'm much better at it now, but back then I just saw a good idea. It did turn out to be a good idea and lots of money came in for the foundation. There were so many details to think about, like how to package the necklace without it tangling in the mail. How to even get enough charms to fill the orders we were receiving, too. So many details that I had not even thought of: shipping labels, post office trips, notes from me thanking them for their orders, donation receipts—so many things.

I enlisted the help of relatives and friends, but it was just too much. When Shayna and Garrett offered to take over, I was so thankful. I felt bad, though, too, because I thought I was putting a burden on them that they didn't want, but it turned out they really wanted to be involved with the foundation and help any way they could. I was overjoyed. Shayna and Garrett streamlined the process and were able to take over the job, much to my relief!

Feeding an ostrich.

Me feeding a zebra.

Where's the Rage, Jaycee?

At Yale University, Rebecca, Abigail, and I were presenting our critique of Stockholm syndrome paper to a panel of mental health professionals. When it was time for questions, I was asked, "Where's the rage, Jaycee?" It came easy for me to say to her, "I choose not to be angry and let Phillip and Nancy consume one more minute of my life." The woman who said this to me felt like she was the angry one and perhaps was looking for someone to reciprocate her anger.

Why? Why do I choose to believe that, act that? Do I ever get angry? Yes, I do. I can be angry at Phillip and Nancy, I can be angry at the incompetence of law enforcement and the government and its role in my daughters' and my further imprisonment. I even can be angry at my daughters at times; they are quite normal and therefore, like most teens, very frustrating for a single mom. There's lots in this world to be angry about. The world is a very angry place, and there are some very angry people living here on this planet we all share. However, I don't choose to live in an angry state all of the time. I don't live there. I don't wallow in self-pity and think of all the "what ifs" of life. It's a waste of my time and energy. That's the choice I have made. It doesn't make sense to me to get angry and stay that way. I don't want to be a mad, angry person.

I have lost friendships over anger. Someone I genuinely cared about and thought was a supporter of mine turned out to be a very angry person and ended up making many assumptions and judgments about me, which never feels good. I have encountered this feeling before but directed at what happened to me, not at me.

The American Legion Child Welfare Foundation had given my foundation a grant. We were asked to come to their annual conference in Baltimore and talk about how we used the grant and how thankful we were. We also had a booth manned by my sister and her husband, Garrett. I sometimes sat at the booth with them to help out. You really find out who remembers you and who doesn't at things like these. A lot of people thought I was Elizabeth Smart and some even thought I was one of the Cleveland women. My sister's husband was great at explaining the foundation and its founder, me. At times I would introduce myself and people would be surprised I was there.

One group came over and listened as the foundation was explained, and when Garrett got to the part about me, a man became visibly angry at what he was hearing of my story. He didn't realize I was sitting there. He said he would like to get ahold of Phillip and put him in a room so the family could have at him.

And then he'd like to have a chance. He was so upset for what we had been through it was actually quite touching for me to see. The man finally asked Garrett one question: "How can she be okay? Is she doing okay these days?" I felt a little shy to stand up and make my presence known after all that, but I did stand up and I said to him, "Hi, and yes, I'm doing quite well, thank you." He was embarrassed for his conduct, but I told him not to be. I understood that he just felt rage for what happened to me and my kids. I appreciated his support. I told him that my girls and I were actually thriving now. There is life after something tragic happens. Life doesn't have to end if you don't want it to. It's all in how you look at it. I hope that man doesn't let his anger consume him and that he felt some relief in seeing how well I was doing.

There was a big orange tree in the backyard of my grandparents' house. When I was little and before the world got scary, I would sit under that tree and look up to the sky and wonder what my life would be like when I grew up. I think we all have those moments as kids. I never imagined I would be kidnapped, imprisoned, and have two kids by the age of seventeen.

I imagined I would be a great writer of fiction and travel all around the world. Or perhaps I would have been a great veterinarian and by the time I was the age I am now, I would have saved the lives of hundreds of animals. I guess the point I'm trying to make is we never know what life has in store for us. Sometimes it's bad and sometimes we win the lotto. Life hits hard. It's the small memories that I hold dearest to me.

It's those little things that kept me going.

Like walks on the beach with my mom, collecting seashells when I was eight. Or holding my new baby sister for the first time. Even memories of watching my own daughters take their first steps and the time my youngest daughter at the age of four made me a cake out of sticks and mud for my twenty-first birthday. Those are the pieces of myself I hold on to that make me glad to be alive.

I've always been a cloud hopper. Sometimes I wish I was a more complicated person. Am I missing something? Should I be some other person than the one I am? Sometimes I think others might feel like I should. I don't know how to be anyone else but me.

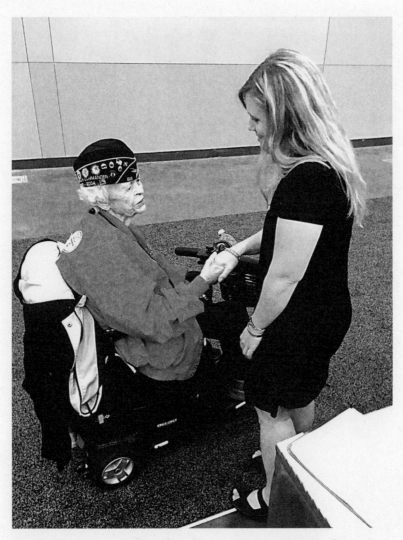

Me meeting a new friend at the American Legion Conference.

Open Wide and Say AHHH!

Going to the dentist was not one of the firsts I was ever looking forward to doing. But after eighteen years with no dental care, I was encouraged to get a checkup. It's true I have no love for the dentist. When I was little I had countless trips to the dentist. My grandma used to fill my bottles with juice, which, as you can guess, wreaked havoc with my baby teeth. As I grew up I was constantly told to brush my teeth. I'm not sure I always listened because by the time Phillip kidnapped me I already had three fillings.

For the first time I didn't have anybody reminding me to brush my teeth. Actually, I didn't have a toothbrush for a really long time. I found myself becoming concerned about my teeth for the first time in my life. It had been drilled into me to brush my teeth twice a day for the longest time that now that I couldn't I felt weird and like a bad girl. I actually wanted to brush my teeth. Really, really badly. I couldn't, though. So I would use my tongue as much as I could to get as much food off them as possible. I would then scrape off the plaque that was accumulating with my fingers and use a napkin to clean them as best I could. The day Phillip gave me more privileges and a toothbrush I was really happy. It feels weird writing about getting the privilege of a toothbrush, but it really was in my situation. I hate that I was thankful to Phillip for this simple basic staple of life. I never thought about how important brushing was until I couldn't do it anymore.

I have also chewed sugarless gum throughout the years, and I think it helps, too. In fact, I learned this neat trick with the dentist. I have been going to the same dentist for these past years, and I notice that when I chew sugarless gum before a cleaning I always get better feedback about my teeth than if I don't chew gum before. I really like when the cleanings go smoothly and fast so I can get out of that dreaded chair faster. I have had only one cavity since my return to the living. When I knew it had to be drilled, I was so not into it. I just told myself that it would be done before I knew it and at least now I could go to the dentist for stuff like this. Whatever I said to myself didn't really work. Ha-ha. I thought, This is going to hurt like hell. I pictured this new dentist using what my old dentist as a child had used. It was this plastic-coated thing that went over my entire mouth and had some strange covering that could be flavored. Grossest thing ever.

My new dentist assured me that he would not be using that. But he knew what I was talking about. He also said I would not feel anything except a little pinch from the Novocain. Guess what? He was right. I did feel the pinch and that did hurt a little, but after that it was mostly just the pressure and the thought of what he was doing that freaked me out. Best of all, no more silver fillings. My new filling matches my teeth perfectly and you can't even tell I have a filling there. My old fillings are all silver but are still in great shape considering no dentist for eighteen years.

Phillip used to go to the colleges that would give dental procedures for free because they were teaching colleges. He had to have a lot of teeth pulled, I think, due to his drug use. He had deep cavities from the missing teeth and often got infections. He would have the worst breath ever because of this. What I hated most was when he would suck on his back teeth to draw out the infection, he said, and then spit it out. His cheeks would get all pulled in when he did this and make him look like a skeleton because he was so thin and gaunt looking. He was always so narcissistic, I wonder what he thought of his mug shot because it was not even attractive. In fact, I never found him attractive in all the years of my captivity. He was a gross man and will die a gross man. I know in prison they have good dental and medical for inmates, so he probably had all the tooth stuff fixed, and I know he had that hideous mole of his removed. Part of me, the mean part, would have liked to see him keep that mole for a while and live with being ugly. Well, I guess he still is, so I win.

Through Thick and Thin

Since I've been back I have been around for many important moments of my best friend Jessie's life and firsts for me, too.

I was there when her mom passed away. I felt like I had lost a piece of myself, too, that day. I remember her mom and all that we did together. Linda would take us to the beach and Knott's Berry Farm. She gave me my first and last glass of eggnog . . . yuck! She helped to tie my shoes and clean my nose when it was runny. She was a very special lady, and when Jessie told me she was gone I didn't quite believe it for a while. I know my grandma Ninny died a short time after I was taken, and I will never get to see her again. Losing Linda was the first time I had someone that close to me die after I had just seen them a few weeks before. It was a blow to the heart. I could not even imagine the heartache of losing your mom. The memorial service that Jessie put together was a nice way to say good-bye and full of good memories that we all shared of her mom.

The next big moment was her wedding. She and Mike decided to have it in his hometown in Minnesota to be close to his parents. They couldn't travel that far, so it was the perfect solution. Jessie's uncle flew them up in his private plane, and Mom and I met them there. We stayed in a little lodge full of big wood posts and carvings on the walls. It was a double wedding because Mike's brother was also getting married and they decided to combine them. I met a new friend that day, the photographer and Jessie's friend, Kassel. She had known Kassel since she was little, and he was a big part of her uncle's life.

We picked out Jessie's dress on a previous visit, and she paired it with an old pair of cowboy boots. The dress was so perfect and fit her to a tee even though we had gotten it at a second-hand dress shop. Jessie asked if my mom would marry them, and she said she'd look into it. Apparently, you can become ordained online—who knew? Mom went through the process online and became an ordained person who could perform marriage ceremonies legally. So cool! She conducted both Jessie and Mike's and his brother's weddings together at the same time. After the vows were said and then the "I do's," it was time for the reception and pictures. Lots and lots of pictures in true Jessie fashion. Did I mention she loves to take pictures? She says she does it so she doesn't miss or forget a moment of her life. Makes sense with memories as old as ours! Oh, and did I mention it was snowing! Like a lot. And guess what. She wanted pictures outside. So in true best-friend fashion, I went outside in the cold without my jacket and posed with her for a few shots. Then ran back in to warm up. It's hard to admit, but the pictures were pretty spectacular with the snow coming down.

After the reception Jessie said she wanted to go to a bar. We were in a very small town, and it was a weird feeling going with her new husband and his best man and Kassel the photographer to a bar for some reason. Jessie got a little tipsy. Well, I was a little tipsy and she was really, really tipsy. She hadn't eaten much because she wanted to fit into her dress, so all the alcohol went straight to her head. Then it came out. I held her hair while she got it all out. We both were laughing so hard by this point I couldn't even see straight. I was laughing so hard my snort came out. What an embarrassing thing to snort when I laugh. That night I played pool for the first time. It was so fun to learn something brand-new. Jessie was a pro. Me not so much, but I liked learning. Mike's best man asked me to dance, and I didn't know how. But he was patient and taught me the steps. It was awkward because he was so tall and I'm not, and it was the first time I danced with a guy, like, ever. Then I danced again with Kassel. It was fun. After that we all went back to the lodge and made angels in the snow. I'm not sure why because it was freaking cold out there, but that's what we did and I liked it!

Next moment came a year after that, and it was the birth of her baby boy. Complete home birth. I was happy she could choose where she would give birth. I didn't have a choice. After listening to all the research out there, I think having her baby at home was a good choice for her and her circumstances. She had it all planned out. She would have the baby at her uncle's guest house. She had the birthing tub already there. I flew down a day before her due date and expected the baby would come any day. I was wrong, like really wrong. This was going to be a late baby. Like a week late. During the "time of waiting," as I like to call it, we tried everything. She went for acupuncture. She ate spicy food, which she hates. We had even heard that walking helps and that if she walked with one leg on the curb and the other down on the street that it would help. She even drank castor oil! Poor thing. I remember that day so well. She had said she was having Braxton Hicks contractions all morning. I had to ask her what that was and she told me false labor. Okay, so she's having some false labor pains, no big deal. That night we had dinner and watched some movie. I went to bed after the movie. It was about ten o'clock. I thought she would go to bed soon, too, so when I heard her come into my room and say, "Can you come be with me?" I was really groggy and confused. I looked at the clock. Midnight. I rubbed my eyes and followed her out into the other room where she's folding laundry. Folding laundry at midnight—girl, what's up? I said and she said she just wanted some company as she doubled over in obvious pain. I'm like, Jessie, are you in labor? And she said, No I think it's just Braxton Hicks. I'm no doctor, but these Braxton Hicks things are lasting a bit longer than I thought they would. Here, she says as she hands me a piece of paper, I've kept track of them. My eyes are still a little grainy, but I look at the paper she gives me and think I'm seeing things. By now the contractions were fifteen minutes apart. Contractions mean labor, not false labor. She didn't look convinced, though. Total denial. I said, Have you called Mike? and she said, no, she didn't want to worry him. Time to call the midwife, I said. Really, she said, and I'm like, yes, right now, as another spasm racks her body! I am not delivering this baby alone! I think to myself. She calls up the midwife and tells her she's having some contractions, nothing too bad. No rush. No rush? Is she crazy? I get on the phone and tell the midwife that her contractions are fifteen minutes apart and she needs to get here now. Like a half hour ago now. Next we call Mike. I hear her calmly telling Mike that she might be in labor but she's not sure and she didn't want him to miss work. I take the phone from her and say, you need to come now. The doula arrives before the midwife, and we get Jessie in a warm bath. She said this would either speed up delivery or relax it a bit and give us more time. The midwife and Mike were still en route.

Did I mention we were upstairs and the birthing tub was downstairs? Yeah, that happened, and guess what else: the stinking warm bath sped things up! Mike arrived after that and helped to get Jessie out of the tub, and we headed downstairs. Halfway down and her water breaks. I really thought I would be in panic mode by now, but I really just felt calm. It was like my body knew I needed to be there for my friend who by this time is moaning like she's dying, and all I could do was film it. Yep, film it because I knew that is what she would want most from this experience— the video of it happening. Something that she couldn't do at the moment. But would if she could. They get her in the tub. By this time the little baby boy's head is crowning. I think to myself, Gosh, how did I do this? Not once but twice. Seeing someone else go through it seems really scary. But at the time I don't re- member really thinking about being scared. I just did what my body was telling me to do and somehow it all ended up okay.

Seeing her in so much pain was hard for me, though, and I just wanted it to be over for her. Looking through the camera lens helped me, believe it or not, because I had a job and a focus.

Finally, the midwife arrived. Just in the nick of time, too, because Mike was about to deliver his own son. What I remember most from those moments was the little guy shot out of his momma like a rocket. So naturally I gave him the nickname of Little Rocket.

I haven't really been around babies in a long time. I do re-member holding each of my daughters for the first time, though. I think it's one of those things that nothing could erase except amnesia. When it was my turn to hold the new little baby boy, I thought I would be really emotional, but although it was a very special moment, it did not make me want another baby. I was happy to hold the little guy but so glad that he had parents to give him back to.

A couple years later I finally felt like I was getting my friend back. She had been so busy with the baby that it seemed she hadn't much time for me. I was happy when she would come up to visit, but sometimes I don't like to share. Little Rocket was growing so big, and it was really fun to watch all the new things he could do each time I saw him.

One day Jessie calls me and says she has something to tell me. It sounded like something important. She took a long pause and I said, "Spit it out. It's not like you're pregnant." Well, if I ever stuck my foot in my mouth it would have been at that moment because the pause just got longer, and I said, "You're pregnant?" And her reply was yesssss.

This baby was a total surprise to her and Mike. Well, yeah, and me, too! I really wanted to be happy for them and I was, but that selfish part of me creeps in sometimes, and all I could think of was, She has years of kids ahead of her.

Again I came down to her house the day before her due date.

I hit a lot of traffic, but I wasn't worried because Little Rocket was so late I thought I had plenty of time. I was wrong. This little one was impatient to be born and came thirty minutes before I arrived. I was so bummed to have missed it. But at the same time I was a little relieved when I got there to have missed all the chaos, because she was a breech birth so the the midwife had to call the paramedics. Apparently, I missed the paramedics and the fire truck that showed up with sirens blaring. The midwife and doula were able to take care of everything and ended up not needing assistance, but the guys wanted to see a baby being born, I guess, and stayed for the entire birth. She had a beautiful baby girl with a ring of firemen around her. Jessie called it the "ring of fire." Just looking at the precious little girl made all my petty jealousies go out the window. Well, most of them.

I feel so privileged to have shared so many important moments of my best friend's life. It's these moments that make all the bad moments seem unimportant. One day we will sit around in our old age and laugh about all the silly, sad, fun, humbling, hilarious, embarrassing times we had with each other, and I am truly looking forward to that day.

Me and best friend Jessie.   *Me and Jessie.*

Me and Jessie.

Me and Jessie.

Me with Jessie's baby.

Now, That's Grand!

Last summer I took a trip to the Grand Canyon with my youngest daughter and my aunt Tina. I had the whole trip planned out. We drove from Southern California to Williams, Arizona. The Grand Canyon Railway package I purchased gave us one night in Williams and then one night in the Grand Canyon and then back to Williams.

I was surprised by all the different weather we encountered on the drive there. One part would get really hot, like 107 degrees, and then it would start raining in other places. Off in the distance you could see storms gathering, but right where we were there would be blue, cloudless skies. It was pretty awesome to see.

I had read about a place called Bearizona and when we got to Williams, we decided to go check it out since we had time. I'm so glad we did. It turned out to be so much fun. It was a wild animal park that was in the Kaibab National Forest. And you could drive through the different habitats of animals. It was home to so many bears all living together in one habitat. As we drove past, we could see bears playing and strolling around. It was really amazing to be so close to the bears, something I never thought I would get to do. We also drove through the wolf habitat where they had a pack of white wolves. One wolf was so curious it tried to pull the bumper from the car in front of us. They have really strong jaws. The other habitats had big bison and longhorn steer and lots of other animals like mountain goats. After our cruise through the forest we entered the zoo area where they take care of the baby animals on foot. I'm not much into zoos for the captivity aspect, but this was a really nice one with a lot of room for the animals. These animals were kind of in their natural habitats. It wasn't like being free, but it was natural in a way to them and they were making the best of their unnatural situation. Kind of like what I did during my captivity.

My favorite part was seeing the baby bear cubs eating their lunch and making all kinds of noise while they munched. I could totally relate.

The next day we boarded the train that would take us to the famous Grand Canyon. I learned that this train also has a Polar Express train in the winter that takes kids to see Santa. The ride took a couple of hours, but they had plenty of entertainment. There was a Wild West show complete with robbers before we boarded the train. Later, they came to try to rob us on the train. It was really funny because if you wanted to be robbed you had to make sure the money was totally visible to the robbers. I decided I didn't want to be robbed. When I was little I remember being so scared of the robbers that came to the Knott's Berry Farm train. I thought they were real. It's nice to know they are not real robbers, but I think they are making it a little too unbelievable these days.

I think in the beginning I might have had more of a reaction to these robbers or maybe not. It's hard to tell now. I can't tell you one thing that made me better. I can't even tell you why I'm not scared of everything in my world. All I can say is I got the best therapy in the world, and I had the best therapist in the world, and I had the best team working with her to help me and my family. I have the best mom, and I have the best family and friends. Even though I went through some very unlucky things, I don't count myself an unlucky person . . . well, mostly. Bad things still happen to me, like the time I burned my back after putting one of those icy hot packs on and sleeping with it overnight. The next morning, I pulled it off and had the worst freezer burn ever. It hurt like crazy. Dumb things happen. Life happens all around us every day. I just deal with every situation, new or not new, with what's in my brain. Some of that is new. Like the skills I learned when working with my friend Jane in the beginning, which really helped me prepare for doing those things by myself. So there's not an easy answer of why I'm okay. I want to be okay and I think that helps a lot. I want to be out there in the world, going to places like Monkey River, Ireland, and the Grand Canyon. Seeing and doing all I can.

From the train we got on a bus that would take us to the canyon. Luckily, I landed a window seat on the bus, so my first sight of the Grand Canyon was not blocked. I remember think-

ing whoever named this landmark was right. It was grand in every
sense of the word. Beautiful colors throughout the different lay-
ers make it look like a painting. In fact, I think it doesn't really
look real. It's just too big to be real.

We decide to walk on one of the trails leading down into the
canyon. I remember one boy commented on my choice of shoes,
thinking they were not appropriate for walking. I chose to differ
with him and said my Skecher sandals were actually quite comfy
and quite adequate for the task. He obviously knew nothing of
shoes.

Tina really wanted to see the sunrise over the canyon. I kind
of wanted to see it, but I didn't want to get up so early. She won
and we arranged to have a taxi pick us up at four in the morning to get us to the lookout we wanted. Our taxi driver wanted
to know our position on desalination. At four in the morning
my opinion was not quite forming. I was still half asleep. I was
really thankful for the sweatshirt I had purchased the night before, because this morning was freezing. Taxi man went from
talking about the state of the ocean water to classic cars in the
blink of an eye. He said he liked to work on classic cars and fix
them up and that his newest project was a 1980 Honda Civic.
I remember looking at my aunt and rolling my eyes and thinking, Gosh, when did 1980 become classic? Wow, I felt old. I
guess I missed more years than I thought and suddenly being
born in 1980 was ancient—well, at least classic—status. I felt
a little like Rip Van Winkle, waking up to this whole new world.
Even though I feel a million years old sometimes, I'm only in
my thirties!

We finally arrived at our spot and it was a little scary being dropped in what felt like the middle of nowhere in the dark. Our eyes adjusted, and we found a spot to sit and wait. Others came and found their spots, too. I guess we weren't the only crazy people who wanted to see the sunrise. As it got lighter out, I could make out more details around me. Looking out over the canyon, though, made me dizzy. I thought I saw the ledge and I thought I could make out the bottom. As it got lighter, though, I realized that it wasn't the bottom and that the bottom was a long, long way down. The sunrise was spectacular and well worth the lost sleep. Having that special moment with my aunt was like eating a really good piece of chocolate cake but without all the calories.

Our next fun thing was a helicopter ride over the Grand Canyon. I took my trusty Dramamine so I wouldn't ruin the experience for myself. I thought it would be scary lifting off, but it was almost like the hot-air balloon ride I took. We just lifted up and it felt very smooth. My daughter was a little nervous at first. She really enjoyed it after she got used to the motion. We could all talk to each other with the headphones they gave us to put on during the flight. The pilot played music related to flying like "Come Fly with Me," by Frank Sinatra, "I Just Wanna Fly," by Sugar Ray, and "Elevation," by U2. A little cheesy, but hey, I like cheesy. Hence my favorite movie being *The Princess Bride*—can't get cheesier than "As you wish" and other great lines that I could probably quote quite easily. As you go over the trees and approach the canyon that one song that goes . . . well, I can't really write it out, but you know the one with the drums. It's from the movie *2001: A Space Odyssey*. Well, anyway that song comes on when you fly over the canyon and it feels like the bottom just drops off underneath you and you get the feeling that all the air has left your lungs. It felt like we were falling, but we weren't and that song is playing. It made it all seem much more dramatic than it really was. Once I recovered and told myself we were still in the air, it was easier to look around. What a sight. There were storms gathering in the distance. You could literally see the rain falling. The bottom of the canyon had a river going through it in places. Everywhere I looked it was just simply beautiful. We saw a couple of hawks or maybe they were eagles flying in circles on the hot air currents. Some of the formations we could just fly right over while others we had to climb to pass. There was even another helicopter that flew close by to us and then went on its way. The whole experience was really cool, and I was sad to have it end after only an hour and half of fly time. It was such a fulfilling, rewarding experience to be in such a beautiful place. I feel like I have seen the canyon by air, and next time I would like to explore the bottom by mule.

Baked Potatoes

One of my kids' pet peeves about me is why I don't give more to homeless people we see on the street. Well, for one, I'm a little afraid of them. It's an irrational fear because I wasn't harmed or kidnapped by a homeless person. I also know that they have lives and families like everybody else and have just fallen on hard times. I guess for me the main thing is I sometimes feel that they don't use the money in the way that I feel would be best. I think I don't fully trust those I don't know. I would much rather know where my money is going and how it is being used. Maybe I'm a control freak. It's weird how some experiences can have a good effect on you and some experiences make you think the worst.

One such experience that I think had more of an impact on me than I thought was one time when what appeared to be a nice-looking man asked me for some groceries. I was going into

Walgreens and thought, Okay, I'm in a public place, safe. Why not help him out a bit? He looked harmless. I told him I would buy him a few things. He went and picked up a few things and I grabbed what I came in for. We entered the checkout line together. As I was paying for the few items he brought, I see him looking at the magazines. He immediately picked up one for 'tweens and remarked, "Wow, these kids look so grown-up." I got a really bad vibe from that and immediately thought, OMG, I just bought groceries for a pedophile! We parted ways at the checkout counter, and I hurried to my car and locked the doors before I drove off. Who knows if he was a pedophile or not? It was just plain creepy. It reminds me not to judge a book by its cover because you never know who a person really is. Even a clean-cut person can harbor secrets. Phillip and Nancy always appeared to be two normal people, but look at all the nasty secrets they were hiding in their backyard—literally! Experiences like this have a tendency to make me think all homeless people are scary, but another time I realized that they do not intend any harm even if they look really scary.

One day Rebecca and I were going into a market. There was a grungy-looking homeless guy on the street, and he asked for some money for a baked potato. Rebecca gave him the money. I told her, "He's not really going to use that for a baked potato." She said, "Maybe he will." He really reminded me of Phillip in appearance in a lot of ways if he ever grew his beard out. Which made me feel really uncomfortable about just being around him. That was my projection, though, and in reality I knew nothing about this guy and judged him on his appearance only. My bad! Because, well, when we came out, that guy was chomping away on his baked potato from Wendy's. I was wrong that day and it really bothered me. Shouldn't I give more? I think the question of how much to give is something we all struggle with. I know I do, but I give in the ways that I can.

I get a lot of fulfillment from the JAYC Foundation and the good we are able to provide for families. We have helped a family recover from the murder of their son. We were able to connect them with Transitioning Families and their animal-assisted program where they got to relax and reconnect after the blow to their family. I think what we give most to families is similar to what it feels like to have a warm, comfy blanket fresh from the dryer wrapped around them so they feel safe to let whatever emotions or feelings running through them out. I think every family needs support and therapy to get them to see that they can be okay again. That they just have a new normal now.

I think running the foundation has made me grow as a person, too. Being the president of anything is not all it's cracked up to be. In fact, it's pretty dang hard. Turning away any family is really hard, but I know we can't help everyone who applies. I have to maintain a budget and careful thought is given to the families that do come up before my board of directors for a vote on whether we can help. I would like to take every case, but being in charge has made me realize that making choices is a part of being in charge. Even the president can't do it all, and each day I am thankful I am surrounded by very good friends and a team that has lasted the test of time. They help me in every way. I think having a foundation that specializes in one area can be good, and it can also be really hard sometimes. Because of this, it can be hard to get funding for something that people don't know a lot about. Nobody really uses "reunification" in their day-to-day lives. To the families we have helped, it is emblazoned in their lives forever. They know how important it is to try to keep their families working together after a major blow.

The JAYC School Groups have become an important aspect of the foundation as well. I think it's important we teach kids how to be caring to one another. My little sister was bullied after I was taken, and when I found out upon my return, that made me really sad to think about her going through that. I am really glad to see this program taking off. We now have the groups in Alabama and New Hampshire. Anything that gets kids working together and cooperating is good in my book. I remember my friend Lanae telling me about a little girl who was kidnapped for four years. She was found and reunited with her parents. Seems like a perfectly nice story with a happy ending. Well, I thought so, too, but it turns out that, meaning well, her parents put this little girl back into the same school she was in before. The students had heard stories throughout the years of the missing girl, and I think they were scared. But that doesn't excuse the constant bullying she received. I thought, Why, if this happened to my sister and now this little girl and who knows who else, why isn't there a program or speakers to go to schools that have experienced a trauma? Because I do think it's traumatizing not only to the family but to the community as well. Kids get scared and sometimes they lash out in mean ways because they don't know any better. The Just Ask Yourself to Care! groups were born from this need I saw in schools. It's a way to incorporate caring, compassion, safety, and attunement to others all in a fun, animal-centered, eight-week journey through the Pony Express. It's fun but it's also learning. It's the best of both worlds.

We have our very own program for law enforcement officers who sometimes get stuck in a rut. A lot of ruts, I think, happened in my case and mistakes were made. The JAYC LEO program centers on giving officers, parole agents, any kind of official, really, a chance to explore and get out of their ruts. It's fun to watch the officers work with horses. Most of them have never been around horses, so this really puts them out of their comfort zones. It makes them better listeners, too, because they don't want to get their feet stepped on. We take the time to talk about self-care, too, because like I always say, you can't take care of others until you take care of you! The team is great at facilitating these workshops and say they are one of the most fulfilling aspects of the foundation just because of the participants' reactions and seeing their eyes open to new possibilities in their line of work. A real transformation of hopefulness enters them and rejuvenates them to do their jobs better. Because let's face it: they have one of the toughest jobs out there.

Pass the Cheese, Please

One of the few times Phillip and Nancy took us out on a trip was to the arboretum in San Francisco. To the average onlookers, these outings probably looked like any ordinary family having a nice picnic on a park bench. In fact, we were anything but ordinary, and Phillip had an ulterior motive for bringing us there. He felt it was a good place to hear the force. The force is what he called the angels he said he could hear. And apparently the big fan generators that were in the park were the perfect conductors of these voices. I always thought he saw *Star Wars* one too many times given his "force" reference. He made us each take a turn with the headphones to see if we could hear it, too. The voices, that is.

So if you ever passed a table with one person wearing head-phones, well, I guess you saw us. It was always so embarrassing to be there. I just wanted to enjoy the semi-freedom of being in the open fresh air, even if I wasn't completely free. At least my daughters got the chance to play around while it wasn't their turn. His quirky behavior was part of our norm, and even though we would roll our eyes to each other when Phillip and Nancy weren't looking, we knew not to act out in any other way. These kinds of outings would last anywhere from an hour to several.

Nancy was always the one to hear it. I wonder if the weed she smoked before had anything to do with it. Anyway, I guess we all make assumptions, and assuming we were a normal everyday family was probably what everyone did that day. I don't blame anyone for that. We all assume. Makes me wonder about what I assume about things that I have seen. Most people never would have thought some psychopath and his crazy wife had us as captives in a million years. Part of that was my fault, but the evil you know is sometimes better than the evil you do not. And he was the evil I knew. I hope this little story does make you wonder, though. Maybe one person or several can be saved a little sooner. We all have the ability to Just Ask Ourselves to Care a little bit more in this life.

My Inner Circle

I have been thinking and thinking: How am I going to end this book? For months I have not had the answer, and I just realized why. Because my life has not ended! How can I end a book if I still feel I have so much to experience? I haven't tipped the top of the iceberg yet—in fact, that sounds really fun. I might have to go to Antarctica for that one day. But every book needs at least some kind of conclusion or something. So what should I write about? What else is there to say? And then I look around . . .

My cat Emma is lying on the couch beside me. Come to think about it, she's been there every day that I have sat here writing. And then there's Zelda; she's there in bed waiting for me every night. She sleeps right by my side without fail. My trusty dog Bull is asleep in his bed. I know come five he will become Mister Annoying and beg for his dinner. I will procrastinate because I want to write one more paragraph, but his beautiful, big, brown eyes will stare at me, his big body will be quivering, and the pull will be too much. He wins. Dinnertime. These make up my faithful inner circle. They are the ones who never judge and are always there. Even when they are not.

I recently lost one of the cats we were able to bring back with us from our captivity in the backyard. His name was Mousey and he was mine for such a short time. A few months ago, he started losing weight rapidly. It was really weird because he was eating all his food and still looked really skinny. Petting him I could feel his backbone. I also noticed that he was throwing up a lot more than just hairballs. I took him to the vet thinking it was just a bad case of worms. I had no doubt the vet could help him. It actually feels so comforting to know I can take my pets to the vet now. No more worrying if they are sick and begging Phillip to take them in. The vet did a check and became concerned with a lump he thought he felt in his abdomen. He recommended an X-ray right away. What about worms? I asked. He didn't think it was worms and suspected Mousey had an obstruction somewhere in his gut. We did the X-ray. He told me there was something there but without exploratory surgery he wouldn't know. Whoa, hold your horses! Surgery? I just came in for some worming medication and you're telling me you want to perform surgery? He said, We could do an ultrasound but that it would be pricey. I said, Okay, let's do the ultrasound. I didn't want my cat being opened up like that and explored. It sounded really scary. He said to take Mousey home and keep him separated from the other cats and see if he poops or pees. He would call when they had the ultrasound equipment. I took him home.

As I was riding my horse the next day, I got a call from the vet. They had run some blood tests on him, too, and the results seemed okay. I could tell he wanted to tell me something else. He said he would like to do another X-ray before the ultrasound. I took Mousey in again and we did another X-ray. The look on the vet's face this time really had me worried. These are the moments I hate in life. Sometimes the look on someone's face says it all. It was the same look my vet gave me before I had to make the decision to put my horse Ed down. He looked at me and said he thought exploratory surgery was best. I didn't want to answer. I knew the choice was mine to make. I could take him home right now. And part of me really wanted to. I wanted to deny this reality. I wanted to live in ignorance of anything wrong with my beloved cat. But I couldn't, and I found myself saying okay. A simple word, but it had such a lasting impact on my life. I picked up my kitty and told him I would be leaving him for a short time and I would be back to pick him up. I left with an empty carrier that day. The vet said the surgery would take several hours and he would call when he had more news. Before I left I had to sign the paper. The dreaded paper I didn't even know existed until that moment. The paper that gives the vet permission to euthanize if he feels it necessary. I signed that paper with glazed-over eyes.

I left to run a few errands. My youngest daughter had her own doctor's appointment and we went to that. I was on my way to pick up some animal supplies when the phone rang. It was the vet. He said Mousey had a very large tumor in his stomach and it extended to his gallbladder. It was big. Massive, really, and he was sorry but there wasn't any hope. No hope? What are you talking about? He said, I'm sorry, but your cat can't be saved. I said, Can I come say good-bye? He said that he would be in so much pain if he woke up like this. I didn't want him to be in pain. I need you to let me put him to sleep, he said. You want to kill my cat, you bastard! is what was going around my head. At that moment, I hated this man and everything he said to me was just lies. I wanted to deny it all. I heard the truth in his voice, though, and I also heard the compassion. He did not want to call me with this news. I was a bit out of breath for some reason and it took a lot to get the answer out of me. I almost whispered it, and he had to ask again. Yes, I said, yes, end his suffering. I'm coming, I said, and hung up. My daughter heard the entire conversation and asked if I was okay. I know she was hurting, too, and I hoped she understood my decision. I was driving, but I reached across with my free hand and took hold of hers.

Driving was hard because my eyes were soaked with tears. I drove to the little vet's office and tried to keep it together. I wanted to say good-bye even though he was gone. The vet let me see the body. It was hard to see him with no life inside him. I laid my hand on him and told him I was back to bring him home like I promised.

That evening I looked everywhere for a shovel. I was going to bury my Mousey in a nice spot I had chosen. Where are the goddamn shovels? I shouted. I couldn't find a shovel anywhere and I was getting angrier and angrier. I finally found a really poor excuse for a shovel and started my digging. That made me mad, too. The digging. My best friend and my aunt Tina were there because Thanksgiving was just a day away. I didn't feel very thankful. I was so mad that I had to even dig that stinking hole for my cat that just had worms, damnit! Why couldn't he have just had worms? I couldn't wrap my brain around the fact I had taken him to the vet to get better and now he was dead. As I was digging, I was crying. Jessie and my daughters offered to help, and I just kept saying, "I don't want to dig this fuckin' hole." After a while it felt good to be taking my anger out on the shovel and stupid hole in a way, and it felt even better when they all just took turns helping me. I got his body and laid it gently in the hole. We covered it with dirt and I made a nice little circle of rocks for the top. I said good-bye. I didn't want to say good-bye.

I wasn't sure if I was going to include this in my book because it is still a fresh memory and hurts my heart, but Mousey was my best kitty friend, and I want to always remember the joy he brought into my life. He was my bathroom buddy. He loved to go into the bathroom with me and would lick my hand. I miss that a lot. He has a brother named Tyson who looks a lot like him, just a little lighter in color but in the dark virtually the same. It's hard seeing him sometimes and not think of my Mousey, but they are very different in personality.

I am so lucky to have so many animal friends in my life. They come in so many shapes, sizes, and colors, and each has their own personality. What they have in common, though, is their ability to make me feel wanted and loved each in their own way. They are my inner circle each and every one of them. I'm sure this circle will grow in the future and at times it will get smaller. Animals have always been a constant in my life, though, from the time I was a little baby and my grandma's gray Persian cat Sugar would keep my head warm in my crib to the time I was three and got my first kitten, Rusty. His favorite resting spot for some reason was my training potty. Thank goodness, I didn't use it anymore because I was a big girl learning to use the big-girl potty.

So my ending for this book is not an ending at all because my life goes on. Life goes on even during the bad, hard, heart-crushing times. Even these moments have taught me something. I'm not thankful for them, but I am tolerant of them because of this fact. I know the constants in my life will always be there even when they feel far away, whether in spirit, memory, or life. I will continue to learn and grow and help those I can. This is how I have rebuilt my life. Little moments. One day at a time. This is the good, bad, and the cheesy life I lead. I will always try to be the best person I can and take advantage of the time I have been granted in this life. My adventure continues, and I hope yours continues, too!

Zelda, Emma, Tyson, and Mousey.

Mousey kissing Zelda.